WILD
GAME
COOKING

WILD GAME
COOKING

OVER 100 RECIPES

FOR VENISON, ELK, MOOSE, RABBIT,
DUCK, FISH & MORE

CIDER MILL PRESS

BOOK PUBLISHERS

CONTENTS

Introduction

There are many reasons one would want to go hunting, but the financial incentive is one that most people overlook.

Even before inflation began carrying food costs to uncomfortable heights, rare was the household that couldn't use a way to cut costs. Well, as seasoned hunters know, heading out into the wilds and harvesting a deer, an elk, or a moose is one of the best ways to meet this call. By bringing home just one of these large animals, a family has enough protein to last them for a year. And, even taking the costs of butchering and storing the animal into account, that provender has been secured far cheaper than they could have managed going to the store.

Add in the considerable satisfaction that comes from supplying your loved ones with sustenance directly through your own efforts, and the peace of mind that attends knowing those ingredients were sourced in the best possible way, and the rewards of incorporating more wild game into one's diet become too powerful to ignore.

But the many benefits of leaning upon the animals one can harvest via hunting also means that one will have to become adept in the kitchen, mastering numerous techniques to ensure that this harvest is honored properly— and that you and your family don't grow tired of eating the particular protein that you brought home.

This book puts you in position to do exactly that. For those times when you're looking to entertain, elegant appetizers and invigorating soups set the stage for a memorable evening. When you're in need of a little comfort, you'll find everything from hearty stews and sauces transform turn your harvest into toothsome, tender morsels to beloved classics like burgers and sandwiches. Should one want to head back out and supplement their haul with birds, rabbits, and fish, there's also plenty of recipes to choose from that feature these smaller and far more plentiful game. There's even a handful of jerky recipes that will keep you going on your next excursion until you've secured your limit.

To deliver such an impressive variety of preparations, the book looks to cuisines around the globe for inspiration, leaning on classic preparations such as b'stilla, vindaloo, curry, algfarsoppa, chili, risotto, and many more standbys that can easily accommodate substitutions and personal preferences. These classics will also teach you how to rely on time-honored techniques such as braising, grilling, and roasting, and determine which ingredients have the ability to stand up to the strong and unique flavors wild game provides.

In short, the recipes here will prove to be an invaluable resource for hunters and cooks of all abilities, providing assurance that their efforts will result in a satisfying end, and plenty of encouragement to head back out into the wilds.

VENISON

Without a doubt, venison is the most popular game that people consume.
It is also the one that requires the most care when preparing,
due to its extremely lean character.

Venison Stew

3 cups ground venison

Salt and pepper, to taste

2 tablespoons extra-virgin olive oil

3 celery stalks, diced

3 potatoes, peeled and cubed

4 carrots, peeled and diced

1½ cups Brussels sprouts, trimmed and halved

1½ cups mushrooms, sliced

2 tablespoons all-purpose flour

1 cup Beef Stock (see page 250)

¾ cup red wine

2 tablespoons red currant jelly

1. Place the venison in a bowl, season it with salt and pepper, and form it into 12 patties.

2. Place the olive oil in a large skillet and warm it over medium heat. Add the venison patties and cook them until they are browned on both sides, about 3 minutes per side. Remove the patties from the skillet and transfer them to a slow cooker.

3. Add the remaining ingredients to the slow cooker, stir to combine, and cook the stew on high until the vegetables are tender, 3 to 4 hours.

4. Ladle the stew into warmed bowls and enjoy.

Venison Risotto

¼ cup extra-virgin olive oil

¾ lb. saddle of venison, diced

Salt and pepper, to taste

1 shallot, finely diced

1 garlic clove, minced

1½ cups Arborio rice

⅔ cup dry white wine

3½ cups Vegetable Stock (see page 251), warm

2 cups diced tomatoes

1 tablespoon chopped fresh rosemary, plus more for garnish

1 teaspoon fresh thyme, plus more for garnish

¾ cup freshly grated Parmesan cheese

2½ tablespoons unsalted butter

1. Place 2 tablespoons of the olive oil in a large skillet and warm it over medium-high heat. Season the venison with salt and pepper, add it to the pan, and sear it until it is browned all over, turning the venison as necessary. Remove the venison from the pan and set it aside.

2. Add the shallot and remaining olive oil to the pan and cook, stirring occasionally, until it is translucent, about 3 minutes. Add the garlic and rice and cook, stirring continually, until the rice gives off a nutty fragrance, 2 to 3 minutes.

3. Add half of the wine and cook, stirring continually, until the rice has absorbed it. Add the remaining wine and cook, stirring, until it has been absorbed.

4. Add the stock a little bit at a time and cook, stirring continually, until each addition has been absorbed by the rice.

5. When the rice is al dente, stir in the tomatoes, rosemary, thyme, Parmesan, butter, and venison, season the risotto with salt and pepper, and cook until warmed through.

6. Garnish the risotto with additional rosemary and thyme and enjoy.

Venison Steaks over Bacon Lentils

For the Lentils

1 cup diced bacon

3 garlic cloves, minced

1 onion, finely diced

2 carrots, peeled and finely diced

1 cup lentils

1 bay leaf

2½ cups Vegetable Stock
(see page 251)

⅔ cup balsamic vinegar

Salt and pepper, to taste

1 tablespoon dried marjoram

2 tablespoons unsalted butter

1 apple, cut into wedges

1 tablespoon chopped fresh parsley

For the Venison

1 tablespoon extra-virgin olive oil

1 tablespoon unsalted butter

1¼ lb. boneless saddle of venison,
cut into medallions

1 sprig of fresh thyme

1 sprig of fresh rosemary

6 tablespoons red wine

2 tablespoons pomegranate seeds,
for garnish

1. Preheat the oven to 350°F. To begin preparations for the lentils, place the bacon in a Dutch oven and cook it over low heat until the fat has rendered, about 3 minutes. Stir in the garlic, onion, and carrots, raise the heat to medium, and cook, stirring continually, for 2 minutes.

2. Drain the lentils, add them to the pot along with the bay leaf, and cook, stirring continually for 1 minute. Add the stock a little bit at a time, replenishing it once it evaporates. Simmer the lentils until they are tender, 20 to 25 minutes.

3. Stir in the balsamic vinegar, salt, pepper, and marjoram and remove the pot from heat.

4. Place the butter in a skillet and melt it over medium heat. Add the apple and cook until it is golden brown, 2 to 4 minutes, turning it as necessary. Remove the apple from the pan and set it aside.

5. To begin preparations for the venison, place the olive oil and butter in a large cast-iron skillet and warm the mixture over medium heat. Add the venison steaks, thyme, and rosemary and sear the steaks until they are browned all over, about 6 minutes, turning them as necessary and occasionally basting them with the pan juices.

6. Transfer the pan to the oven and cook the steaks until they are medium-rare, 6 to 8 minutes. Remove the steaks from the oven, transfer them to a plate, and cover them with aluminum foil.

7. Add the red wine to the pan and bring it to a boil over high heat, scraping up any browned bits from the bottom of the pan. Strain the reduction over the steaks and garnish them with the pomegranate seeds.

8. Place the lentils in a serving dish and stir in the parsley and browned apple wedges. Serve the lentils alongside the steaks.

VENISON

Venison Jerky

2 lb. venison roast

2 tablespoons brown sugar

2 tablespoons liquid smoke

¼ cup tamari or soy sauce

2 teaspoons kosher salt

1½ teaspoons black pepper

2 tablespoons
Worcestershire sauce

2 teaspoons paprika

1. Trim the roast to remove any excess fat and silverskin. Cut the meat into strips that are between ⅛ and ¼ inch thick, slicing with the grain for a chewier jerky or against the grain for a more tender jerky.

2. Place the remaining ingredients in a mixing bowl and whisk until the sugar has dissolved and the mixture is thoroughly combined.

3. Add the meat to the marinade and stir until the strips are evenly coated.

4. Cover the bowl with plastic wrap, place it in the refrigerator, and marinate for at least 6 hours. If time allows, let the meat marinate overnight.

5. Remove the meat from the refrigerator and give it a stir.

6. To prepare the jerky in a dehydrator, arrange the meat on the dehydrator trays, making sure to leave space between each piece. Place it in the dehydrator, set the temperature to 160°F, and dehydrate until the meat has dried out but is still flexible, 4 to 6 hours.

7. To prepare the jerky in an oven, preheat the oven to 175°F. Line two rimmed baking sheets with aluminum foil and place wire racks over the foil. Arrange the strips of meat on the racks, making sure to leave space between each piece and to keep the meat in a single layer. Place the pans in the oven and bake for 1½ hours. Rotate the pans and then bake until the meat is dry to the touch, leathery, and slightly chewy, 1½ to 2½ hours.

8. Store the jerky at room temperature in an airtight container, where it will keep for a few weeks. If you are interested in a longer shelf life for your jerky, place it in a bag and vacuum seal it. Stored in a cool, dry place, the vacuum-sealed jerky will keep for 6 months to 2 years.

Teriyaki Venison Jerky

2 lb. venison roast

2 tablespoons brown sugar

2 tablespoons liquid smoke

¼ cup tamari or soy sauce

2 teaspoons kosher salt

1½ teaspoons black pepper

¼ cup teriyaki sauce

1. Trim the roast to remove any excess fat and silverskin. Cut the meat into strips that are between ⅛ and ¼ inch thick, slicing with the grain for a chewier jerky or against the grain for a more tender jerky.

2. Place the remaining ingredients in a mixing bowl and whisk until the sugar has dissolved and the mixture is thoroughly combined.

3. Add the meat to the marinade and stir until the strips are evenly coated.

4. Cover the bowl with plastic wrap, place it in the refrigerator, and marinate for at least 6 hours. If time allows, let the meat marinate overnight.

5. Remove the meat from the refrigerator and give it a stir.

6. To prepare the jerky in a dehydrator, arrange the meat on the dehydrator trays, making sure to leave space between each piece. Place it in the dehydrator, set the temperature to 160°F, and dehydrate until the meat has dried out but is still flexible, 4 to 6 hours.

7. To prepare the jerky in an oven, preheat the oven to 175°F. Line two rimmed baking sheets with aluminum foil and place wire racks over the foil. Arrange the strips of meat on the racks, making sure to leave space between each piece and to keep the meat in a single layer. Place the pans in the oven and bake for 1½ hours. Rotate the pans and then bake until the meat is dry to the touch, leathery, and slightly chewy, 1½ to 2½ hours.

8. Store the jerky at room temperature in an airtight container, where it will keep for a few weeks. If you are interested in a longer shelf life for your jerky, place it in a bag and vacuum seal it. Stored in a cool, dry place, the vacuum-sealed jerky will keep for 6 months to 2 years.

VENISON

SAFETY FIRST

When working with meat, one must take the time and precautions to ensure that the process remains hygienic. When preserving meat, this becomes even more important. The following rules will keep you safe when making jerky, and guarantee the best results:

- Wash your hands before and after handling raw meat.

- Make sure you have a working surface that is clean and disinfected.

- Refrigerate raw meat at 40°F or below.

- If you are planning to use meat that is frozen, make sure to thaw the meat in the refrigerator, not on the kitchen counter.

- When marinating the meat, store it in the refrigerator. Do not reuse any marinade.

- If you are preparing jerky from wild game, make sure the hunter followed safe practices and that the animal was dressed properly.

- Let the meat come to a temperature of 160°F when drying it, as this will help decrease the possibility of bacterial growth.

- The thickness of the strips makes a difference. It is recommended not to slice the meat into strips any thicker than ¼ inch.

- Trim all the fat from the meat. It can become rancid and spoil the jerky.

If you follow these rules, you're well on your way to making quality jerky at home.

Peppered Venison Loin Steaks with Red Wine Shallots

4 venison loin steaks (about 6 oz. each), gently pounded thin

8 strips of bacon

½ teaspoon kosher salt, plus more to taste

2 tablespoons crushed peppercorns

2 tablespoons canola oil

4 sprigs of fresh rosemary

2 cups dry red wine

¼ cup sugar

3 tablespoons balsamic vinegar

8 small shallots

4 tablespoons unsalted butter, cubed

1. Preheat the oven to 350°F. Wrap 2 strips of bacon around each steak and secure the bacon with kitchen twine. Season the steaks with the salt and press the crushed peppercorns firmly into both sides of the steaks.

2. Place the canola oil in a large cast-iron skillet and warm it over medium-high heat. Add the steaks and sear them until they are browned on both sides, 3 to 4 minutes for each side.

3. Add the rosemary to the pan, transfer the steaks to the oven, and roast them until their interiors are 145°F, 10 to 15 minutes, basting them with the pan juices occasionally.

4. Remove the steaks from the oven, transfer them to a plate, and cover them loosely with aluminum foil.

5. Place the skillet over medium heat and add the red wine, sugar, and balsamic vinegar to the pan. Bring the mixture to a boil, scraping up any browned bits from the bottom of the pan with a wooden spoon. Add the shallots, reduce the heat, and simmer the mixture until the shallots are tender and the sauce is syrupy, about 2 minutes.

6. Whisk the butter into the sauce a cube at a time. Season the sauce with salt and serve it alongside the steaks.

Venison Ragout

2½ lbs. venison, trimmed and cubed

Salt and pepper, to taste

3 tablespoons all-purpose flour

¼ cup extra-virgin olive oil

4 strips of bacon, chopped

2 onions, finely diced

3 large carrots, peeled and finely diced

2 celery stalks, finely diced

2 garlic cloves, minced

⅔ cup dry white wine

½ teaspoon dried oregano

½ teaspoon dried basil

2 bay leaves

3 cups Beef Stock (see page 250)

½ cup heavy cream

1 lb. spaghetti

1. Season the venison with salt and pepper. Place the flour in a shallow bowl and dredge the venison in it.

2. Place 2 tablespoons of olive oil in a Dutch oven and warm it over medium heat. Working in batches to avoid crowding the pot, add the venison and sear it until it is browned all over, turning it as necessary. If the pan starts to look dry, add more of the remaining olive oil. Remove the seared venison from the pot and set it aside.

3. Add the bacon to the pot and cook, stirring occasionally, until it is crispy and golden brown. Remove the bacon from the pot and set it aside.

4. Add the remaining olive oil to the pot and warm it. Add the onions, carrots, and celery, season the mixture with salt, and cook, stirring occasionally, until the vegetables are golden brown and soft, about 10 minutes.

5. Stir in the garlic and cook for 1 minute. Add the wine, bring the mixture to a simmer, and cook until the liquid has reduced by three-quarters.

6. Add the dried herbs and bay leaves, return the venison and bacon to the pot, and stir to combine. Pour in the stock and bring the sauce to a boil. Partially cover the pot, reduce the heat to low, and cook, stirring occasionally, until the venison is so tender it can be pulled apart with your fingers, 1½ to 2 hours.

7. While the sauce is simmering, bring salted water to a boil in a large saucepan. Add the spaghetti and cook until it is al dente, 6 to 8 minutes. Drain the spaghetti and set it aside.

8. Stir the cream into the sauce and bring it to a simmer. Season the sauce with salt and pepper and serve it over the spaghetti.

VENISON

Roast Venison with Mashed Potatoes & Celeriac

1. Preheat the oven to 325°F. To begin preparations for the venison, place the olive oil in a large cast-iron skillet and warm it over medium heat. Season the venison with salt and pepper, add it to the pan, and sear it until it is browned all over, turning it as necessary.

2. Add the garlic and rosemary to the pan, cover it, place it in the oven, and roast the venison until it is cooked through, 15 to 20 minutes.

3. Place the cranberry sauce, confectioner's sugar, and tomato paste in a medium saucepan and warm the mixture over medium heat for 2 minutes, stirring frequently. Add the wine, bring it to a simmer, and cook until it has reduced slightly. Add the onion, carrot, celeriac, and stocks and cook the mixture over low heat until the vegetables are tender, about 1 hour.

4. Strain the sauce, return it to the pan, and add the allspice berries, bay leaves, juniper berries, and citrus peels. Cook the sauce until it has reduced by half and strain it into a clean saucepan.

5. Stir in the cornstarch and chocolate and cook until the sauce has thickened slightly. Season the sauce with salt and pepper and set it aside.

6. To begin preparations for the mashed potatoes and celeriac, place the potatoes and celeriac in a saucepan, cover them with water, and bring it to a boil. Cook until they are tender, about 15 minutes, drain the vegetables, and transfer them to a mixing bowl.

7. Mash the potatoes and celeriac until they are smooth. Stir in the cream, butter, and nutmeg, season the mixture with salt and pepper, and serve it alongside the venison and the sauce.

For the Venison

1 tablespoon extra-virgin oil

1 lb. venison tenderloin

Salt and pepper, to taste

1 garlic clove, chopped

1 sprig of fresh rosemary

2 tablespoons cranberry sauce
(see page 49)

1 teaspoon confectioner's
sugar

2 tablespoons tomato paste

¾ cup dry red wine

1 onion, chopped

1 carrot, peeled and chopped

¼ celeriac, peeled and
chopped

4 cups Venison Stock
(see page 252)

4 cups Vegetable Stock
(see page 251)

1 teaspoon allspice berries

2 bay leaves

1 teaspoon juniper berries

1 strip of lemon peel

1 strip of orange peel

1 tablespoon cornstarch

1 teaspoon dark chocolate

For the Mashed Potatoes
& Celeriac

1¼ lbs. potatoes, peeled
and diced

½ lb. celeriac, peeled and diced

¼ cup heavy cream

3 tablespoons unsalted butter

Pinch of freshly grated
nutmeg

Salt and pepper, to taste

Hunters' Stew with Venison & Lentils

3 tablespoons all-purpose flour

Salt and pepper, to taste

2¾ lbs. venison, cubed

2 tablespoons extra-virgin olive oil

2 onions, chopped

2 carrots, peeled and chopped

2 bay leaves

⅔ cup red lentils

½ cup dry red wine

4 cups Venison Stock (see page 252)

2 tablespoons unsalted butter

6 oz. mushrooms

Fresh rosemary, chopped, for garnish

1. Preheat the oven to 300°F. Place the flour in a shallow bowl, season it with salt and pepper, and stir to combine. Dredge the venison in the seasoned flour.

2. Place the olive oil in a Dutch oven and warm it over medium heat. Working in batches to avoid crowding the pot, add the venison and cook until it is browned all over, turning it as necessary. Remove the venison from the pot and set it aside.

3. Add the onions and carrots to the pot and cook, stir occasionally, until they have softened, about 5 minutes.

4. Return the venison to the pot, add the bay leaves, lentils, wine, and stock and bring the stew to a boil. Cover the pot, place it in the oven, and braise the stew until the venison is very tender, 2 to 2½ hours.

5. Place the butter in a large skillet and melt it over medium heat. Add the mushrooms in an even layer and cook until they are browned all over, stirring once or twice.

6. Remove the stew from the oven, place the mushrooms on top, garnish with the rosemary, and serve.

Venison Loin with an Olive Crust & Caraway Brittle

1. Preheat the oven to 250°F. To prepare the brittle, place the sugar and water in a small skillet and warm the mixture over medium heat, stirring to dissolve the sugar. Add the caraway seeds and warm the mixture until the sugar caramelizes. Pour the mixture onto a piece of parchment paper and let it set.

2. To begin preparations for the olive crust, place all of the ingredients, except for the brown sugar, in a food processor and blitz until the mixture is a smooth, thick paste. Place the mixture between two sheets of parchment paper and roll it out until it is ¼ inch thick. Place the crust in the refrigerator.

3. To begin preparations for the cabbage, place the olive oil in a large saucepan and warm it over medium heat. Add the cabbage and cook, stirring occasionally, until it softens slightly.

4. Add the caraway seeds and sparkling wine to the pan, cover it, and reduce the heat to low. Cook the cabbage until it is tender, about 10 minutes. Remove the pan from heat and keep it covered.

5. To begin preparations for the venison, place the Clarified Butter in a large cast-iron skillet and melt it over high heat. Add the thyme, elderberries, bay leaves, and venison and sear it until it is browned all over, turning it as necessary. Cover the pan, place it in the oven, and roast until it is cooked to the desired level of doneness, about 15 minutes for medium-rare.

6. Remove the pan from the oven, transfer the venison to a plate, and cover it with aluminum foil. Deglaze the skillet with the red wine, scraping up any browned bits from the bottom of the pan. Add the stock, bring the mixture to a boil, and cook until it has reduced by half. Stir in the butter then remove the sauce from heat.

7. Set the oven's broiler to high and line a baking sheet with parchment paper. Place the venison on the baking sheet. Cut the olive crust into 4 pieces and place one piece on top of each piece of venison. Sprinkle the brown sugar over the crust, place the venison in the oven, and broil until the sugar has caramelized.

8. Divide the cabbage among the serving plates. Top each portion with a piece of venison and some of the brittle and then drizzle the sauce over the top. Garnish with thyme and enjoy.

For the Brittle

¼ cup sugar

1 teaspoon water

1 tablespoon caraway seeds

For the Olive Crust

½ cup black olives, pits removed

¾ cup bread crumbs

¾ cup unsalted butter, softened

2 egg yolks

Salt and pepper, to taste

2 tablespoons brown sugar

For the Cabbage

2 tablespoons extra-virgin olive oil

10 cups shredded green cabbage

1 teaspoon caraway seeds

5 oz. sparkling wine

For the Venison

2 tablespoons Clarified Butter (see page 256)

2 sprigs of fresh thyme

2 tablespoons dried elderberries

4 bay leaves

2 lb. venison tenderloin, cut into 4 pieces

6 tablespoons dry red wine

1¼ cups Venison Stock (see page 252)

2 tablespoons unsalted butter

Fresh thyme, for garnish

Venison Pot Pie

1½ lbs. venison steaks

2 tablespoons extra-virgin olive oil

1 large onion, diced

3 garlic cloves, minced

6 carrots, peeled and chopped

3 cups sliced mushrooms

6 Red Bliss potatoes, rinsed well and diced

1 teaspoon dried thyme

1 teaspoon dried oregano

1 teaspoon dried rosemary

3 cups Beef Stock (see page 250)

1 tablespoon cornstarch

2 tablespoons milk

Salt and pepper, to taste

1 teaspoon Worcestershire sauce

2 sheets of frozen puff pastry, thawed

1 egg, beaten

1. Rinse the venison under cold water and pat it dry with paper towels. Place 1 tablespoon of the olive oil in a Dutch oven and warm it over medium heat. Working in batches to avoid crowding the pot, add the venison and sear it until it is browned all over, turning it as necessary. Remove the seared venison from the pot and set it aside.

2. Add the onion and remaining olive oil to the pot and cook, stirring occasionally, until it is translucent, about 3 minutes. Add the garlic, carrots, mushrooms, and potatoes and cook, stirring frequently, until the vegetables have softened, about 8 minutes.

3. Add the dried herbs and stock and return the venison to the pot. Cover the pot and simmer the mixture until the venison is fork-tender, 1½ to 2 hours.

4. Preheat the oven to 350°F. Place the cornstarch and milk in a small bowl and whisk to combine. Add the slurry to the pot, raise the heat to medium-high, and cook until the sauce has thickened. Season the filling with salt and pepper, stir in the Worcestershire sauce, and remove the pot from heat.

5. Divide the filling among two 9-inch pie plates or one large baking dish and place a sheet of puff pastry over each portion. Trim away any excess dough and pinch the edge to seal the pot pies. Brush the puff pastry with the beaten egg, cut several small slits in the top, and place the pot pies in the oven.

6. Bake the pot pies until the crusts are golden brown, 25 to 30 minutes. Remove the pot pies from the oven and let them cool briefly before serving.

VENISON

Braised Venison with Creamed Cabbage

1. Preheat the oven to 350°F. To begin preparations for the venison, season the venison with salt and pepper. Place 2 tablespoons of butter in a large skillet and melt it over medium heat. Add the venison and sear it until it is browned all over, turning it as necessary.

2. Remove the venison from the pan and press the crushed peppercorns and juniper berries into it. Wrap the venison with the bacon and secure the bacon with kitchen twine.

3. Place the remaining butter in a Dutch oven and melt it over medium heat. Add the onion, carrot, celeriac, and leek and cook, stirring occasionally, until the vegetables have softened, about 5 minutes.

4. Add the venison to the pot, pour the red wine over it, and bring it to a simmer. Add the stock and sugar, cover the Dutch oven, and place it in the oven. Braise the venison until it is very tender, 1½ to 2 hours.

5. Remove the venison from the oven and let it rest, covered, for 20 minutes.

6. To begin preparations for the cabbage, bring a large saucepan of water to a boil. Add the cabbage and salt and boil the cabbage for 3 minutes. Drain the cabbage, run it under cold water, and let it drain again.

7. Place the butter in a large skillet and melt it over medium heat. Add the onion and cook, stirring occasionally, until it is translucent, about 2 minutes. Add the bacon and cook, stirring occasionally, until it is browned, 6 to 8 minutes.

8. Add the cabbage, stock, and cream, reduce the heat to medium-low, and cook until the liquid has reduced slightly, about 6 minutes.

9. Season the cabbage with salt and pepper, stir in the nutmeg, and serve it alongside the venison.

For the Venison

2½ lb. venison haunch, deboned and rolled

Salt and pepper, to taste

4 tablespoons unsalted butter

1 tablespoon black peppercorns, lightly crushed

1 tablespoon juniper berries, lightly crushed

12 strips of bacon

1 onion, chopped

1 carrot, peeled and chopped

1 celeriac, trimmed, peeled, and chopped

1 leek, trimmed, rinsed well, and sliced

½ cup red wine

2 cups Venison Stock (see page 252)

Pinch of sugar

For the Cabbage

1 medium savoy cabbage, shredded

Salt, to taste

2 tablespoons unsalted butter

1 onion, sliced thin

4 strips of bacon, finely diced

6 tablespoons Chicken Stock (see page 253)

¾ cup heavy cream

Pinch of freshly grated nutmeg

Bacon-Wrapped Leg of Venison

3 lb. boneless leg of venison

1 tablespoon kosher salt

4 tablespoons unsalted butter

12 strips of bacon

1 tablespoon black peppercorns, lightly crushed

1 tablespoon juniper berries, lightly crushed

1 onion, chopped

1 carrot, peeled and chopped

1 leek, trimmed, rinsed well, and sliced

½ cup dry red wine

2 cups Beef Stock (see page 250)

Pinch of sugar

1. Preheat the oven to 350°F. Rinse the venison under cold running water and pat it dry with paper towels. Season it with the salt.

2. Place half of the butter in a large cast-iron skillet and melt it over medium heat. Add the venison and sear it until it is browned all over, turning it as necessary. Remove the seared venison from the pan and wrap the bacon around it. Secure the bacon with kitchen twine and sprinkle the peppercorns and juniper berries over the bacon, pressing down so that they adhere.

3. Place the remaining butter in the skillet and melt it over medium heat. Add the onion, carrot, and leek and cook, stirring occasionally, until the vegetables have softened, about 5 minutes.

4. Return the venison to the pan, pour the wine over it, and bring the wine to a boil. Stir in the stock and sugar, cover the skillet, and place it in the over. Braise the venison until it is fork-tender, 1½ to 2 hours.

5. Remove the venison from the oven, transfer it to a cutting board, and let it rest for 10 minutes before slicing and serving with the vegetables.

Venison Filets with Brussels Sprouts & Chanterelles

1½ lb. venison loin

Salt and pepper, to taste

2 tablespoons canola oil

1 lb. Brussels sprouts, trimmed and leaves separated

2 tablespoons unsalted butter

10 oz. chanterelle mushrooms

1 garlic clove, minced

1 tablespoon chopped fresh parsley

1 teaspoon chopped fresh rosemary

Pinch of freshly grated nutmeg

Sour cream, for serving

1. Preheat the oven to 250°F. Pat the venison dry with paper towels and cut it into four pieces. Season the venison with salt and pepper.

2. Place the canola oil in a large cast-iron skillet and warm it over medium heat. Add the venison and sear it until it is browned all over, turning it as necessary.

3. Place the skillet in the oven and roast until the venison is medium, 25 to 30 minutes.

4. While the venison is in the oven, bring salted water to a boil in a large saucepan and prepare an ice bath. Add the Brussels sprouts to the boiling water and cook for 1 minute. Drain the Brussels sprouts, plunge them into the ice bath, and then drain them again.

5. Place the butter in a large skillet and melt it over medium heat. Add the mushrooms and cook for 3 minutes. Add the garlic, parsley, rosemary, nutmeg, and Brussels sprouts, season the mixture with salt and pepper, and reduce the heat to medium-low. Cook, stirring occasionally, until everything is warmed through.

6. Remove the venison from the oven and let it rest for 10 minutes before slicing and serving with the vegetables and sour cream.

Venison Goulash

⅓ cup all-purpose flour

2 lbs. boneless venison shoulder, trimmed and cubed

Salt and pepper, to taste

3 tablespoons extra-virgin olive oil

2 tablespoons unsalted butter

3 large carrots, peeled and diced

1 onion, finely diced

2 garlic cloves, minced

¾ cup dry red wine

2 teaspoons paprika

2 bay leaves

¾ cup tomato puree

3 cups Beef Stock (see page 250)

¾ cup red currants

Classic Dumplings (see page 268)

1. Place the flour in a shallow dish, dredge the venison in the flour, and season it with salt and pepper.

2. Place the olive oil in a Dutch oven and warm it over medium heat. Working in batches to avoid crowding the pot, add the venison and sear it until it is browned all over. Transfer the seared venison to a plate and set it aside.

3. Add the butter to the pot and melt it. Add the carrots, onion, garlic, and a pinch of salt and cook, stirring frequently, until the vegetables have softened, about 8 minutes.

4. Deglaze the pot with the red wine, scraping up any browned bits from the bottom of the pot. Cook until the wine has reduced by three-quarters and then return the venison to the pan. Stir in the paprika, bay leaves, passata, stock, and red currants and bring the goulash to a boil.

5. Reduce the heat so that the goulash gently simmers and cook until the venison is extremely tender, about 2 hours, stirring occasionally.

6. Remove the goulash from heat and cover the pot.

7. Fill a saucepan halfway with water and bring it to a simmer. Place the dumplings in a steaming basket, place the basket over the simmering water, and steam the dumplings until they are cooked through, about 10 minutes.

8. Serve the dumplings alongside the goulash.

Venison Escalopes with Shallots in Red Wine

3 tablespoons Clarified Butter (see page 256)

2½ lbs. venison steaks, pounded thin

Salt and pepper, to taste

2 tablespoons chopped fresh rosemary

2 cups dry red wine

¼ cup sugar

2 tablespoons balsamic vinegar

8 shallots, halved

6 tablespoons unsalted butter, cubed

Mashed potatoes (see page 68), for serving

1. Preheat the oven to 200°F. Place the Clarified Butter in a large skillet and melt it over medium-high heat. Season the venison steaks with salt and pepper. Working in batches to avoid crowding the pan, add the venison steaks to the pan and cook until they are browned on both sides and just medium-rare, about 2 minutes, turning them over just once. Transfer the steaks to a platter, sprinkle the rosemary over the top, and place them in the oven to keep them warm.

2. Deglaze the pan with the red wine, scraping up any browned bits from the bottom of the pan. Stir in the sugar and vinegar, bring the sauce to a boil, and add the shallots. Reduce the heat to low heat and cook until the sauce is syrupy and the shallots are tender, about 20 minutes.

3. Stir in the butter and serve the shallots and sauce alongside the steaks and mashed potatoes.

YIELD: 4 TO 6 SERVINGS / **ACTIVE TIME:** 1 HOUR / **TOTAL TIME:** 3 HOURS

Braised Venison with Cranberry Sauce

⅓ cup all-purpose flour

2 lbs. boneless venison shoulder, trimmed and cubed

Salt and pepper, to taste

3 tablespoons extra-virgin olive oil

2 tablespoons unsalted butter

1 large onion, finely diced

2 carrots, peeled and finely diced

2 celery stalks, sliced

2 garlic cloves, minced

2 tablespoons tomato paste

⅔ cups dry red wine

1 Bouquet Garni
(see page 267)

1¾ cups Beef Stock
(see page 250)

1½ cups cranberries

¼ cup sugar

Zest and juice of ½ orange

2 tablespoons sour cream

2 teaspoons fresh thyme

1. Preheat the oven to 300°F. Place the flour in a shallow bowl and dredge the venison in it. Season the venison generously with salt and pepper.

2. Place 1 tablespoon of olive oil in a Dutch oven and warm it over medium heat. Working in batches to keep from crowding the pot, add the venison and sear it until it is browned all over, turning it as necessary and adding more of the olive oil with each batch. Transfer the browned venison to a plate and set it aside.

3. Add the butter and melt it over medium-low heat. Add the onion, carrots, celery, garlic, and a pinch of salt and cook, stirring frequently, until the vegetables have softened, about 8 minutes.

4. Stir in the tomato paste and cook for 2 minutes. Deglaze the pot with the red wine, scraping up any browned bits from the bottom. Cook until the red wine has reduced by three-quarters. Return the venison to the pot, along with any juices.

5. Add the Bouquet Garni and stock and bring the mixture to a boil. Cover the Dutch oven and place it in the oven. Braise the venison until it is very tender, about 2½ hours.

6. Place the cranberries, sugar, orange zest, and orange juice in a saucepan and cook the mixture over medium heat, stirring occasionally, until the cranberries start to collapse, 15 to 20 minutes. Remove the cranberry sauce from heat and let it cool briefly.

7. Remove the venison from the oven, stir in the sour cream and thyme, and season it with salt and pepper. Serve alongside the cranberry sauce.

VENISON

49

Venison Bourguignon

3 lbs. venison shoulder, trimmed and cubed

3 tablespoons extra-virgin olive oil

4 large shallots, chopped

4 strips of bacon, chopped

2 garlic cloves, minced

2 cups dry red wine

1 cup Beef Stock (see page 250)

1 teaspoon fresh thyme

2 bay leaves

Salt and pepper, to taste

2 tablespoons unsalted butter

2 cups button mushrooms

2 cups small chanterelle mushrooms

Fresh parsley, chopped, for garnish

1. Preheat the oven to 325°F. Place the olive oil in a Dutch oven and warm it over medium heat. Working in batches to avoid crowding the pot, add the venison and sear it until it is browned all over, turning it as necessary. Remove the browned venison from the pot and set it aside.

2. Add the shallots and bacon to the pot and cook, stirring occasionally, until they are lightly browned. Add the garlic, return the venison to the pot, and cook, stirring frequently, for 2 minutes.

3. Deglaze the pot with the wine and stock, scraping up any browned bits from the bottom. Bring the dish to a boil, add the thyme and bay leaves, and season it with salt and pepper.

4. Cover the pot, place it in the oven, and cook until the venison is very tender, 2½ to 3 hours.

5. Remove the Dutch oven from the oven, leave the cover on, and let the stew rest.

6. Place the butter in a large skillet and melt it over medium heat. Working in batches to avoid crowding the pan, add the mushrooms and cook until they are browned all over, stirring occasionally.

7. Stir the mushrooms into the stew, garnish it with parsley, and enjoy.

Venison Burgers

1 lb. ground venison

½ lb. ground sausage

1 teaspoon kosher salt

1 teaspoon black pepper

1 tablespoon extra-virgin olive oil

½ cup mayonnaise

2 tablespoons Rose Hip Syrup (see page 269)

4 hamburger buns

½ cup chopped red cabbage

8 strips of bacon, cooked

½ cup dried cranberries

¼ cup crispy onions (see page 100)

1. Place the venison, sausage, salt, and pepper in a large mixing bowl and work the mixture with your hands until it is just combined. Form the mixture into 4 patties.

2. Place the olive oil in a large skillet and warm it over medium-high heat. Add the burgers to the pan and cook until browned on one side, about 4 minutes.

3. Flip the burgers over and cook until they are cooked through, 4 to 5 minutes. Remove the burgers from the pan and let them rest for 2 minutes.

4. Place the mayonnaise and syrup in a small bowl and stir until well combined. Spread some of the mayo on the cut sides of the buns and assemble the burgers with the cooked patties, cabbage, bacon, cranberries, and crispy onions.

Venison Vindaloo

2 tablespoons minced fresh ginger

3 garlic cloves, minced

5 whole cloves

¼ teaspoon cardamom seeds

1 cinnamon stick

2 teaspoons turmeric

1 teaspoon cayenne pepper

¼ cup white wine vinegar

2 teaspoons kosher salt, plus more to taste

2 lbs. boneless venison rump roast, trimmed and cubed

¼ cup ghee or Clarified Butter (see page 256)

1 teaspoon mustard seeds

¼ lb. pearl onions

2 tablespoons Kashmiri chili powder

¼ cup water

2 bay leaves

2 tablespoons chopped scallion greens

Pear & Cranberry Chutney (see page 276), for serving

1. Place the ginger, garlic, cloves, cardamom seeds, cinnamon stick, turmeric, cayenne, vinegar, and salt in a large mixing bowl and stir to combine. Add the venison, toss to coat, and let it marinate for 30 minutes.

2. Place the ghee in a large cast-iron skillet and warm it over medium-high heat. Add the mustard seeds and cook, stirring occasionally, until they start to pop, about 2 minutes. Add the baby onions, season them with salt, and cook, stirring occasionally, for 10 minutes.

3. Remove the venison from the marinade and add it to the pan. Stir in the chili powder, water, and bay leaves and cover the pan. Cook until the venison is cooked through, about 20 minutes.

4. Stir in the scallions and serve the vindaloo with the chutney.

Venison Chops with Apples & Red Currants

4 thick venison chops

2 teaspoons kosher salt

4 tablespoons unsalted butter

1½ cups red wine

2 tablespoons peppercorns, lightly crushed

¼ cup sugar

2 tablespoons balsamic vinegar

½ cup water

1 apple, core removed, sliced

¼ cup red currants, for garnish

Fresh thyme, for garnish

1. Preheat the oven to 250°F. Season the venison with salt. Place the butter in a large cast-iron skillet and warm it over medium heat. Add the venison and sear until it is browned on both sides, turning the chops just once. Transfer the seared venison to a plate and set it aside.

2. Reduce the heat to medium and deglaze the pan with the wine, scraping up any browned bits from the bottom. Stir in the peppercorns, sugar, vinegar, and water and let the liquid come to a boil. Reduce the heat to low and let the liquid simmer until it has reduced by half, about 15 minutes.

3. Return the venison to the skillet and transfer the pan to the oven. Cook the venison for 10 minutes.

4. Add the apple slices to the pan, baste the venison and the apples with the sauce, and cook until the venison is medium-rare, about 10 minutes.

5. Remove the pan from the oven, garnish the dish with the red currants and thyme, and enjoy.

Venison Rump Roast with Brassicas

4 lb. venison rump roast

¼ cup brown sugar

1 tablespoon smoked paprika

1 tablespoon garlic powder

1 tablespoon kosher salt

1 teaspoon black pepper

5 cups Vegetable Stock (see page 251)

1½ cups purple cauliflower florets

1½ cups broccoli florets

1½ cups Brussels sprouts, trimmed and halved

¼ cup all-purpose flour

½ cup white currants

1. Pat the venison dry with paper towels and place it on a rimmed baking sheet. Place the brown sugar, paprika, garlic powder, salt, and pepper in a bowl and stir to combine. Rub the mixture into the venison, cover it with plastic wrap, and chill it in the refrigerator overnight.

2. Preheat the oven to 325°F. Place the venison in a Dutch oven, add 1 cup of stock, cover the pot, and place it in the oven. Braise the venison until the internal temperature is 135°F, about 1½ hours.

3. Remove the venison from the oven and let it rest in the covered Dutch oven.

4. Bring water to a boil in a large saucepan and add the purple cauliflower, broccoli, and Brussels sprouts. Cover the pan and cook until the vegetables are tender, about 8 minutes. Leave the vegetables in the covered pan.

5. Remove ¼ cup of the juices from the Dutch oven and place them in a saucepan. Warm them over medium-high heat, sprinkle the flour over them, and whisk continually for 3 minutes. Add the currants and remaining stock and cook, whisking continually, until the gravy has thickened to the desired consistency.

6. Slice the venison, serve it alongside the vegetables, and pour the gravy over the top.

Tagliatelle with Venison Meatballs

2 tablespoons extra-virgin olive oil

1 onion, finely diced

2 garlic cloves, minced

1 lb. ground venison

1 cup bread crumbs

1 egg, beaten

Salt and pepper, to taste

4 tablespoons unsalted butter

2 cups wild mushrooms

½ teaspoon smoked sweet paprika

1 tablespoon tomato paste

1 tablespoon all-purpose flour

1½ cups Beef Stock (see page 250)

½ cup brandy

½ cup sour cream

1 lb. tagliatelle

Fresh parsley, chopped, for garnish

1. Place 1 tablespoon of the olive oil in a large skillet and warm it over medium-high heat. Add the onion and cook, stirring occasionally, until it has softened, about 5 minutes.

2. Add the garlic and cook, stirring continually, for 1 minute. Transfer the mixture to a large mixing bowl and let it cool slightly.

3. Add the venison, bread crumbs, and egg to the bowl, season the mixture with salt and pepper, and work the mixture with your hands until it is well combined. Form the mixture into approximately 30 small meatballs.

4. Place the remaining olive oil in a clean, large skillet and warm it over medium-high heat. Working in batches to avoid crowding the pan, add the meatballs and cook until they are browned all over and completely cooked through, 8 to 10 minutes, turning them as necessary. Transfer the cooked meatballs to a plate and cover them with aluminum foil.

5. Add the butter to the skillet and raise the temperature to high. Add the mushrooms and cook until they start to brown, about 8 minutes, stirring once or twice.

6. Bring salted water to a boil in a large saucepan. Stir the paprika, tomato paste, and flour into the skillet and cook for 1 minute. Add the stock and brandy and cook until the sauce thickens, about 5 minutes.

7. Return the meatballs to the pan and stir in the sour cream. Cook the sauce for another 5 to 8 minutes.

8. Add the tagliatelle to the boiling water and cook it until it is al dente, 6 to 8 minutes.

9. Drain the pasta, add it to the sauce, and toss to combine. Garnish the dish with fresh parsley and enjoy.

ELK & MOOSE

Elk and moose are less commonly consumed than venison, but no
less wonderful. These comforting recipes help you make the most of
their unique, satisfying flavors.

Algfarssoppa

2 tablespoons extra-virgin olive oil

1 lb. elk shoulder, trimmed and diced

Salt and pepper, to taste

2 onions, diced

1 red bell pepper, stem and seeds removed, diced

1 yellow bell pepper, stem and seeds removed, diced

2 tablespoons tomato paste

4 cups Beef Stock (see page 250)

1 bay leaf

1 teaspoon paprika

½ bunch of fresh basil, chopped

2 tablespoons sour cream, for garnish

1. Place the olive oil in a large saucepan and warm it over medium heat. Season the elk with salt and pepper, place it in the pan, and cook until it is browned all over, turning it as necessary.

2. Add the onions and bell peppers to the pan and cook, stirring occasionally, until the onions are translucent, about 3 minutes.

3. Add the tomato paste and stir until it coats the mixture in the pan. Deglaze the pan with the stock, scraping up any browned bits from the bottom of the pan.

4. Add the bay leaf and paprika, bring the stew to a simmer, and cook until the elk is tender, about 1 hour.

5. Season the stew with salt and pepper, stir in the basil, and ladle the stew into warmed bowls. Top each portion with a dollop of sour cream and enjoy.

Elk with Mashed Potatoes & Cabbage

1. To begin preparations for the cabbage, place the butter in a large saucepan and melt it over medium heat. Add the cabbage and leek and cook, stirring occasionally, until they have softened, about 6 minutes.

2. Add the remaining ingredients and bring the mixture to a simmer. Reduce the heat to low and braise the cabbage until it is very tender, about 40 minutes.

3. To begin preparations for the mashed potatoes, place the potatoes in a saucepan, cover the mixture with water, and season it with salt. Bring the water to a boil and cook the potatoes until they are tender, about 20 minutes. Drain the potatoes and set them aside.

4. To begin preparations for the burgers, place the bread crumbs, elk, egg, and mustard in a bowl, season the mixture with salt and pepper, and work it with your hands until it is thoroughly combined. Shape the mixture into 4 patties.

5. Place the Clarified Butter in a large skillet and melt it over medium-high heat. Add the elk burgers and cook until they are browned on both sides and cooked through, about 8 minutes. Remove the burgers from the skillet, transfer them to a plate, and cover them with aluminum foil.

6. Add the raisins and tomato paste to the skillet and cook, stirring frequently, for 2 minutes. Add the stock to the pan and bring the mixture to a simmer. Cook until the liquid has reduced slightly, about 10 minutes.

7. Place the potatoes in a bowl, add the milk and butter, and mash the mixture until it is smooth. Season the mashed potatoes with salt and the nutmeg and divide them among the serving plates.

8. Top each portion with some of the cabbage and an elk burger, ladle the sauce over the top, and enjoy.

For the Cabbage

2 tablespoons unsalted butter

6 cups sliced green cabbage

½ leek, trimmed, rinsed well, and sliced

1 bay leaf

2 allspice berries

½ cup dry white wine

½ cup Vegetable Stock (see page 251)

Salt and pepper, to taste

For the Mashed Potatoes

1½ cups peeled and diced potatoes

Salt, to taste

½ cup milk

3 tablespoons unsalted butter

Pinch of freshly grated nutmeg

For the Burgers

2 tablespoons bread crumbs

21 oz. ground elk shoulder

1 egg

1 teaspoon Dijon mustard

Salt and pepper, to taste

2½ tablespoons Clarified Butter (see page 256)

½ cup raisins

1 tablespoon tomato paste

1¼ cups Beef Stock (see page 250)

Moose Meatloaf

2 lbs. ground moose

1 onion, diced

2 garlic cloves, minced

1 tablespoon Worcestershire sauce

2 eggs

½ cup bread crumbs

1 tablespoon kosher salt

2 teaspoons black pepper

10 strips of bacon

1. Preheat the oven to 350°F. Line a baking sheet with parchment paper. Place all of the ingredients, except for the bacon, in a mixing bowl and work the mixture with your hands until it is just combined.

2. Turn the mixture out onto the baking sheet and mold it into a 9 x 5–inch loaf.

3. Arrange the bacon slices on top of the loaf, overlapping them slightly and tucking them under the loaf to prevent them from curling in the oven.

4. Place the meatloaf in the oven and bake it until the internal temperature is 165°F.

5. Remove the meatloaf from the oven and let it rest for 10 minutes before slicing and serving.

Elk Jerky

2 lb. elk roast

2 tablespoons brown sugar

2 tablespoons liquid smoke

¼ cup tamari or soy sauce

2 teaspoons kosher salt

1½ teaspoons black pepper

2 tablespoons Worcestershire sauce

2 teaspoons paprika

1. Trim the roast to remove any excess fat and silverskin. Cut the meat into strips that are between ⅛ and ¼ inch thick, slicing with the grain for a chewier jerky or against the grain for a more tender jerky.

2. Place the remaining ingredients in a mixing bowl and whisk until the sugar has dissolved and the mixture is thoroughly combined.

3. Add the meat to the marinade and stir until the strips are evenly coated.

4. Cover the bowl with plastic wrap, place it in the refrigerator, and marinate for at least 6 hours. If time allows, let the meat marinate overnight.

5. Remove the meat from the refrigerator and give it a stir.

6. To prepare the jerky in a dehydrator, arrange the meat on the dehydrator trays, making sure to leave space between each piece. Place it in the dehydrator, set the temperature to 160°F, and dehydrate until the meat has dried out but is still flexible, 6 to 8 hours.

7. To prepare the jerky in an oven, preheat the oven to 175°F. Line two rimmed baking sheets with aluminum foil and place wire racks over the foil. Arrange the strips of meat on the racks, making sure to leave space between each piece and to keep the meat in a single layer. Place the pans in the oven and bake for 1½ hours. Rotate the pans and then bake until the meat is dry to the touch, leathery, and slightly chewy, 1½ to 2½ hours.

8. Store the jerky at room temperature in an airtight container, where it will keep for a few weeks. If you are interested in a longer shelf life for your jerky, place it in a bag and vacuum seal it. Stored in a cool, dry place, the vacuum-sealed jerky will keep for 6 months to 2 years.

Spicy Elk Jerky

2 lbs. elk roast

2 tablespoons brown sugar

2 tablespoons hickory-flavored liquid smoke

2 teaspoons kosher salt

1½ teaspoons black pepper

2 teaspoons hot sauce

1. Trim the roast to remove any excess fat and silverskin. Cut the meat into strips that are between ⅛ and ¼ inch thick, slicing with the grain for a chewier jerky or against the grain for a more tender jerky.

2. Place the remaining ingredients in a mixing bowl and whisk until the sugar has dissolved and the mixture is thoroughly combined.

3. Add the meat to the marinade and stir until the strips are evenly coated.

4. Cover the bowl with plastic wrap, place it in the refrigerator, and marinate for at least 6 hours. If time allows, let the meat marinate overnight.

5. Remove the meat from the refrigerator and give it a stir.

6. To prepare the jerky in a dehydrator, arrange the meat on the dehydrator trays, making sure to leave space between each piece. Place it in the dehydrator, set the temperature to 160°F, and dehydrate until the meat has dried out but is still flexible, 6 to 8 hours.

7. To prepare the jerky in an oven, preheat the oven to 175°F. Line two rimmed baking sheets with aluminum foil and place wire racks over the foil. Arrange the strips of meat on the racks, making sure to leave space between each piece and to keep the meat in a single layer. Place the pans in the oven and bake for 1½ hours. Rotate the pans and then bake until the meat is dry to the touch, leathery, and slightly chewy, 1½ to 2½ hours.

8. Store the jerky at room temperature in an airtight container, where it will keep for a few weeks. If you are interested in a longer shelf life for your jerky, place it in a bag and vacuum seal it. Stored in a cool, dry place, the vacuum-sealed jerky will keep for 6 months to 2 years.

Elk Filets with Roasted Vegetable Cake

1. To begin preparations for the roasted vegetable cake, preheat the oven to 375°F. Place the cream, milk, garlic, and rosemary in a saucepan and bring it to a simmer. Remove the pan from heat and let the mixture steep for 15 minutes.

2. Coat a baking dish with the butter, add the vegetables, season them with salt and pepper, and toss to combine.

3. Strain the cream over the vegetables, cover the baking dish tightly with aluminum foil, and place it in the oven. Bake for 1 hour.

4. Remove the foil and bake the vegetables until the top is golden brown, about 15 minutes.

5. Remove the vegetables from the oven and cover the cake with aluminum foil.

6. To begin preparations for the elk, season the steaks with salt. Place the thyme and cinnamon in a food processor and pulse until they are finely ground. Rub the powder and half of the red currants into the steaks.

7. Warm a cast-iron skillet over medium heat. Coat the pan with 2 tablespoons of the butter and then add the steaks. Cook until seared on both sides and medium-rare, about 8 minutes, turning them over halfway through. Transfer the steaks to a plate and cover them with aluminum foil.

8. Deglaze the pan with the red wine, scraping up any browned bits from the bottom. When the wine has reduced by half, add the stock, 1 tablespoon of butter, and the remaining red currants and cook until the sauce has reduced slightly. Remove the pan from heat and set the sauce aside.

9. Place the remaining butter in a clean skillet and melt it over medium heat. Add the mushrooms in an even layer and cook until they are browned all over, stirring once or twice.

10. Cut the roasted vegetable cake into triangles and serve alongside the elk, mushrooms, and pan sauce.

For the Roasted Vegetable Cake

1½ cups heavy cream

1½ cups whole milk

3 garlic cloves, minced

2 sprigs of fresh rosemary

1 tablespoon unsalted butter, softened

4 cups peeled and grated potatoes

3 cups peeled and grated sweet potatoes

1 large celeriac, peeled and grated

Salt and pepper, to taste

For the Elk

4 elk filets (about 6 oz. each)

Salt, to taste

2 teaspoons fresh thyme

2 cinnamon sticks, crushed

⅔ cup red currants, crushed

5 tablespoons unsalted butter

6 tablespoons red wine

½ cup Beef Stock (see page 250)

1 cup brown mushrooms, halved

Elk Soup with Gnocchi

2 tablespoons extra-virgin olive oil

3 lbs. elk bones
(neck or back bones)

5 cups water

2 bay leaves

3 allspice berries

½ teaspoon kosher salt, plus more to taste

2 tablespoons bread crumbs

¾ lb. ground elk shoulder

1 egg

Black pepper, to taste

Paprika, to taste

½ celeriac, peeled and diced

3 carrots, peeled and diced

3 cups mushrooms

1 onion, diced

4 Roma tomatoes, diced

Gnocchi (see page 270)

Fresh parsley, chopped, for garnish

Pita Bread (see page 271), for serving

1. Place the olive oil in a large saucepan and warm it over medium-high heat. Add the elk bones and cook, stirring occasionally, until they are starting to brown.

2. Add the water, bay leaves, allspice, and salt and bring the mixture to a simmer. Cook for 2 hours, skimming off any impurities that rise to the top.

3. Strain the stock into a clean saucepan and bring it to a simmer.

4. Place the bread crumbs, elk, and egg in a bowl, season the mixture with salt, pepper, and paprika, and work the mixture with your hands until it is thoroughly combined. Form the mixture into small balls and add them to the stock along with the celeriac, carrots, mushrooms, onion, and tomatoes. Bring the soup to a simmer and cook for 10 minutes.

5. Add the Gnocchi to the soup and cook until the meatballs and Gnocchi are cooked through, 5 to 7 minutes.

6. Ladle the soup into warmed bowls, garnish each portion with parsley, and serve with Pita Bread.

Moose Chili

1½ lbs. moose, trimmed and cubed

2 tablespoons extra-virgin olive oil

Salt and pepper, to taste

1 onion, diced

4 garlic cloves, minced

1 (14 oz.) can of diced tomatoes, with their juices

1 cup Tomato Sauce (see page 275)

2 tablespoons chili powder

1 teaspoon cumin

½ teaspoon smoked paprika

2 teaspoons chopped chipotles in adobo

6 oz. tomato paste

½ cup sour cream

½ cup shredded Monterey Jack cheese

¼ cup chopped fresh cilantro

Lime wedges, for serving

1. Season the moose meat with salt and pepper. Place the olive oil in a Dutch oven and warm it over medium-high heat. Add the moose meat and sear it until it is browned all over, turning it as necessary.

2. Add the onion and garlic and cook, stirring continually, for 2 minutes.

3. Stir in the tomatoes, Tomato Sauce, chili powder, cumin, paprika, and chipotles in adobo. Reduce the heat to low, cover the pot, and simmer the chili, stirring occasionally, for 2 hours.

4. Stir in the tomato paste and cook until the moose meat is very tender and the chili's flavor has developed to your liking, 1 to 1 ½ hours.

5. Ladle the chili into warmed bowls, top each portion with some of the sour cream, Monterey Jack, and cilantro, and serve with lime wedges.

Elk Cordon Bleu

¼ cup full-fat Greek yogurt

1 tablespoon Dijon mustard

1 lb. elk loin, sliced into 4 steaks

Salt and pepper, to taste

4 slices of ham

4 slices of Swiss cheese

2 eggs, beaten

1 cup bread crumbs

1. Preheat the oven to 400°F and coat a 13 x 9–inch baking dish with nonstick cooking spray. Place the yogurt and mustard in a mixing bowl and stir to combine. Set the mixture aside.

2. Place each piece of elk between 2 pieces of plastic wrap and pound it to ¼ inch thick. Season the elk with salt and pepper and spread the yogurt mixture over it.

3. Lay a slice of ham on top of the sauce and then top the ham with a slice of the cheese. Fold the elk in half, over the ham and cheese.

4. Place the eggs in a bowl. Place the bread crumbs in a separate bowl. Dredge the elk in the eggs and then in the bread crumbs until they are completely coated. Transfer the elk to the prepared baking dish and place it in the oven.

5. Roast the elk until the interior is 145°F. Remove the elk from the oven and let it rest for 3 minutes before slicing and serving.

Elk Filets with Potato Dauphinoise

For the Potato Dauphinoise

3 large Yukon Gold potatoes, peeled and sliced

1 tablespoon kosher salt

2 teaspoons black pepper

½ cup grated Gruyère cheese

1½ cups heavy cream

¼ teaspoon freshly grated nutmeg

4 tablespoons unsalted butter

½ lb. mushrooms, sliced

For the Elk

1 tablespoon extra-virgin olive oil

4 tablespoons unsalted butter

1 lb. elk loin

1 teaspoon kosher salt

½ teaspoon black pepper

½ teaspoon dried rosemary

½ teaspoon red pepper flakes

½ cup red wine

½ cup Beef Stock (see page 250)

½ cup red currants

1 teaspoon cinnamon

2 tablespoons sugar

1. Preheat the oven to 400°F. Coat a 9-inch pie plate with nonstick cooking spray. To begin preparations for the potato dauphinoise, layer the potatoes in the pie plate, seasoning each layer with the salt and pepper and sprinkling the Gruyère over it.

2. Place the heavy cream and nutmeg in a bowl, whisk to combine, and pour the cream over the potatoes.

3. Cover the pie plate with parchment paper, pressing down on the potatoes to flatten them. Cover the pie plate with aluminum foil and place it in the oven.

4. Bake the dauphinoise until the potatoes are tender, about 1 hour.

5. While the dauphinoise is in the oven, begin preparations for the elk. Place the olive oil and butter in a large cast-iron skillet and warm the mixture over medium-high heat. Add the elk and sear it until it is browned on both sides, turning it as necessary. Reduce the heat to medium, baste the elk with the liquid in the pan, and sprinkle the salt, pepper, rosemary, and red pepper flakes over it.

6. Cook the elk for another 2 minutes, transfer it to a plate, and cover it with aluminum foil.

7. Deglaze the pan with the wine and stock, scraping up any browned bits from the bottom. Reduce the heat to medium-low and let the liquid simmer for 8 minutes.

8. Stir the currants, cinnamon, and sugar into the sauce and simmer for another 5 minutes. Remove the pan from heat and cover.

9. Resume preparations for the dauphinoise. Place the butter in a large skillet and melt it over medium heat. Add the mushrooms and cook, stirring once or twice, until they start to brown, about 8 minutes.

10. Remove the parchment paper and aluminum foil from the dauphinoise and bake it for another 5 minutes to brown the top. Remove the dauphinoise from the oven and top it with the mushrooms.

11. Top the elk with the red currant sauce and serve it alongside the dauphinoise.

Tjälknöl

3 lb. boneless moose rump roast, frozen

8 cups water

½ cup kosher salt

½ cup sugar

2 tablespoons allspice berries, crushed

2 tablespoons juniper berries, crushed

2 tablespoons peppercorns, crushed

4 bay leaves

1. Preheat the oven to 200°F. Place the frozen moose roast on a rack in a shallow roasting pan. Place the pan in the oven and roast until the moose has the desired level of doneness, 7 to 10 hours. The internal temperature of the roast should be 125°F for rare, 135°F for medium-rare, and 145°F for medium.

2. While the moose is in the oven, place the remaining ingredients in a large saucepan and bring the mixture to a boil. Remove the pan from heat and let the brine cool completely.

3. Remove the roast from the oven and place it in large container with a lid. Pour the brine over the roast, making sure it is completely submerged. Cover the container and brine the roast in the refrigerator overnight.

4. Remove the roast from the brine and pat it dry with paper towels. Slice the roast and serve.

Moose Stew

3 tablespoons extra-virgin olive oil

2 lbs. boneless moose short ribs, cubed

Salt and pepper, to taste

4 tablespoons unsalted butter

1 large onion, chopped

2 garlic cloves, minced

¼ cup all-purpose flour

1½ cups red wine

2 tablespoons juniper berries, crushed

1 teaspoon dried thyme

1 bay leaf

2 teaspoons soy sauce

¼ cup black currant jelly

4 cups Mushroom Stock (see page 254)

½ lb. wild mushrooms

¼ cup red currants

1½ cups sour cream

Fresh parsley, chopped, for garnish

1. Place the olive oil in a Dutch oven and warm it over medium-high heat. Season the moose with salt and pepper, add it to the pan, and sear it until it is browned all over. Transfer the moose to a plate and set it aside.

2. Add the butter to the pot and melt it. Add the onion and cook, stirring occasionally, until it is translucent, about 3 minutes. Stir in the garlic and cook, stirring continually, for 1 minute.

3. Return the moose to the pot, add the flour, and stir until everything is evenly coated. Add the wine and cook, stirring occasionally, until the liquid reduces slightly, about 4 minutes.

4. Stir in the juniper berries, thyme, bay leaf, soy sauce, and jelly and then add the stock in a slow stream, stirring continually. Bring the stew to a simmer, reduce the heat to low, and cover the Dutch oven. Cook the stew until the moose is very tender, about 1½ hours.

5. Stir in the mushrooms and red currants and cook the stew for another 10 minutes. Stir in the sour cream, garnish the stew with parsley, and serve.

Elk with Vinegar & Roasted Red Peppers

1 red bell pepper

4 tablespoons unsalted butter

2 lbs. elk top sirloin

Salt and pepper, to taste

4 garlic cloves, chopped

½ cup fresh parsley, chopped

2 tablespoons extra-virgin olive oil

¼ cup red wine vinegar

1. Preheat the oven to 425°F. Place the bell pepper in the oven and roast it until it is charred all over, turning it as necessary. Remove the bell pepper from the oven, place it in a bowl, and cover it with a kitchen towel. Let the pepper steam for 10 minutes, then remove the skin, stem, and seeds, and chop the remaining flesh. Set the roasted red pepper aside.

2. Place the butter in a large cast-iron skillet and melt it over medium-high heat. Season the elk with salt and pepper, add it to the pan, and sear it until it is browned all over, turning it as necessary.

3. Stir in the garlic, parsley, and roasted red pepper, drizzle the olive oil and vinegar over the dish, and transfer the pan to the oven. Roast the elk until the internal temperature reaches 145°F.

4. Remove the elk from the oven and let it rest for 10 minutes before slicing and serving.

Grilled Elk Liver with Beet Salad

2 medium beets

1 tablespoon chopped fresh parsley

1 tablespoon white wine vinegar

2 tablespoons unsalted butter

¼ cup capers, drained

¼ cup crystallized ginger

½ cup white wine

8 slices of elk liver (each ½ inch thick)

Salt and pepper, to taste

2 tablespoons extra-virgin olive oil

1 tablespoon fresh lemon juice

1. Preheat the oven to 400°F. Place the beets in a baking dish, add a few tablespoons of water to the dish, and cover it with aluminum foil. Place the beets in the oven and roast them until they are tender, about 1 hour.

2. Remove the beets from the oven, let them cool, and then peel and dice them. Place the beets in a bowl, add the parsley and vinegar, and stir to combine. Set the beet salad aside.

3. Place the butter in a saucepan and melt it over medium-high heat. Add the capers, ginger, and wine and bring the sauce to a simmer. Reduce the heat to medium and let the sauce simmer for 5 minutes.

4. Season the elk liver with salt and pepper and brush the slices with the olive oil and lemon juice.

5. Warm a grill pan over high heat. Working in batches to avoid crowding the pan, add the elk liver and sear until it is browned, about 2 minutes per side.

6. Transfer the elk liver to a serving dish, spoon the caper sauce over it, and serve it alongside the beet salad.

Elk Curry

1 lb. elk stew meat, trimmed and cubed

Salt and pepper, to taste

2 tablespoons avocado oil

1 onion, diced

4 garlic cloves, minced

1 tablespoon grated fresh ginger

½ teaspoon cinnamon

¼ teaspoon cayenne pepper

3 tablespoons curry powder

3 cups unsweetened coconut milk

¼ cup full-fat yogurt, for garnish

Fresh parsley, chopped, for garnish

Naan (see page 274), for serving

1. Season the elk with salt and pepper. Place the avocado oil in a large skillet and warm it over medium-high heat. Add the elk and sear it until it is browned all over, turning it as necessary. Transfer the elk to a plate and set it aside.

2. Add the onion to the skillet and cook, stirring occasionally, until it has softened, about 5 minutes. Add the garlic, ginger, cinnamon, cayenne, and curry powder and cook, stirring continually, for 1 minute.

3. Add the coconut milk and bring the curry to a simmer. Reduce the heat to low, return the elk to the pan, and cover it. Simmer until the elk is fork-tender, about 2 hours.

4. Ladle the curry into warmed bowls, garnish each portion with yogurt and parsley, and serve with Naan.

Elk Burgers

2 small onions, sliced into thin rings

1 egg, beaten

2 tablespoons all-purpose flour

Salt and pepper, to taste

2 lbs. ground elk

2 tablespoons extra-virgin olive oil

6 slices of cheddar cheese

6 hamburger buns

1 large tomato, sliced thin

¼ cup capers, drained, for garnish

12 gherkins, for garnish

1. Prepare a gas or charcoal grill for medium-high heat (about 450°F). Preheat the oven to 450°F. Line a baking sheet with parchment paper.

2. Place the onions and egg in a mixing bowl and stir to combine. Sprinkle the flour over the onions, season them with salt and pepper, and toss to coat.

3. Transfer the onions to the baking sheet in an even layer. Place them in the oven and bake until they are crispy, about 15 minutes.

4. Place the elk in a large mixing bowl, add the olive oil, and season the mixture with salt and pepper. Work the mixture with your hands until combined and then form it into 6 patties.

5. Place the burgers on the grill and cook them until they are browned on each side and cooked through, 10 to 12 minutes, turning them over halfway through. Place the cheddar cheese on the burgers when they have a few minutes left.

6. Remove the burgers from the grill and remove the crispy onions from the oven. Assemble the burgers with the buns, tomato, crispy onions, capers, and gherkins.

Elk Stew with Juniper Berries & Blue Cheese

2 tablespoons extra-virgin olive oil

1½ lbs. elk stew meat, trimmed and cubed

Salt and pepper, to taste

3 tablespoons unsalted butter

3 shallots, diced

½ lb. chanterelle mushrooms

2 cups dry white wine

3 cups Mushroom Stock (see page 254)

1 teaspoon juniper berries

2 tablespoons all-purpose flour

¼ cup water

2 large carrots, peeled and thickly sliced

2 large potatoes, peeled and cubed

1 bay leaf

½ lb. blue cheese, crumbled

Fresh parsley, chopped, for garnish

1. Place the olive oil in a Dutch oven and warm it over medium-high heat. Season the elk with salt and pepper, add it to the pot, and sear it until it is browned all over, turning it as necessary.

2. Add the butter to the pot and melt it. Add the shallots and mushrooms and cook, stirring occasionally, until they start to soften, about 5 minutes.

3. Stir in the wine, stock, and juniper berries. Place the flour and water in a measuring cup, whisk until the mixture is smooth, and then stir it into the pot.

4. Add the carrots, potatoes, and bay leaf, bring the stew to a boil, and reduce the heat to low. Simmer the stew until the elk is tender, about 1½ hours.

5. Stir in the blue cheese, garnish the stew with fresh parsley, and enjoy.

Grilled Elk Roulade

1½ lbs. elk roast, trimmed and butterflied

Salt and pepper, to taste

8 cloves of Roasted Garlic (see page 255), mashed

2 tablespoons chopped fresh parsley

1 cup red wine

1 cup Beef Stock (see page 250)

8 juniper berries

Fresh rosemary, for garnish

1. Prepare a gas or charcoal grill for medium-high heat (about 450°F), setting up one section for direct heat and another for indirect. Season the elk with salt and pepper. Place the garlic and parsley in a small bowl and stir to combine. Spread the mixture evenly over the elk. Roll the elk up tightly and secure it with kitchen twine every 2 inches or so.

2. Place the elk over direct heat and cook it until it is browned all over, about 10 minutes, turning it as necessary.

3. Place the elk over indirect heat and cook it until the internal temperature is 130°F. Remove the elk from the grill and let it rest for 10 minutes.

4. Place the wine, stock, and juniper berries in a medium saucepan and bring the mixture to a boil. Reduce the heat to medium and simmer until the mixture has reduced by one-third.

5. Slice the elk, spoon the reduction over it, garnish with rosemary, and enjoy.

GAME BIRDS

Though they are more difficult to rely on as an everyday food source, sprinkling a few game birds into the mix is never a bad idea for the cook who hunts. As their flavors are also more interesting than the famously mild taste of chicken, they are worthwhile for all epicures to try out.

Grilled Quail with Tahini & Lemon Sauce

4 quail, cleaned

1 teaspoon peppercorns

1 teaspoon fennel seeds

1 teaspoon chopped fresh rosemary

½ cup extra-virgin olive oil

Salt, to taste

½ cup tahini paste

3½ tablespoons water

2 tablespoons fresh lemon juice

1 garlic clove, minced

1 red chile pepper, stem and seeds removed, sliced

1. Place the quail on a cutting board, breast side down, and use a pair of kitchen shears to remove the backbone. Flip the quail over and press down to flatten them. Rinse the quail under cold water, pat dry with paper towels, and set them aside.

2. Use a mortar and pestle to grind the peppercorns and fennel seeds into a fine powder. Place the powder in a resealable plastic bag, add the rosemary, olive oil, salt, and quail, and shake to coat the quail. Place the quail in the refrigerator and marinate for 1 hour, turning them over halfway through.

3. Prepare a gas or charcoal grill for medium-high heat (about 450°F). Remove the quail from the bag and place them on the grill. Cook until the interior temperature of the quail is 160°F, 5 to 7 minutes, turning them once or twice. Remove the quail from the grill, transfer them to a plate, and cover loosely with aluminum foil.

4. Place the remaining ingredients in a bowl, whisk until the sauce is smooth and creamy, and season it with salt. Drizzle the sauce over the quail and enjoy.

Roast Woodcock with Blueberry Stuffing & Roasted Garlic

1. To begin preparations for the stuffing, place 2 tablespoons of the butter in a skillet and melt it over medium heat. Add the onion and cook, stirring occasionally, until it has softened, about 5 minutes. Add the parsley and garlic and cook, stirring continually, for 1 minute.

2. Add two-thirds of the bread to the skillet and cook until it is golden brown and crispy, stirring occasionally and adding some of the remaining butter if the pan starts to look dry.

3. Place the remaining bread and the milk in a bowl and let the mixture soak.

4. Place the remaining butter in the work bowl of a stand mixer fitted with the paddle attachment and beat the butter until it is soft and smooth. Add the egg and egg yolk and beat until incorporated. Add the bread mixture from the skillet, the soaked bread, and the blueberries and fold to combine. Season the stuffing with salt and pepper and set it aside.

5. Preheat the oven to 425°F. To begin preparations for the woodcock, rinse the birds inside and out and then pat them dry with paper towels.

6. Place the butter in a large skillet and melt it over medium heat. Working with one bird at a time, add the woodcocks to the skillet and sear them on each side for about 1 minute. Remove the seared woodcocks from the pan and fill them with the blueberry stuffing.

7. Place the woodcocks in a roasting pan, season them with salt and pepper, and sprinkle the thyme over the top. Drizzle any pan drippings over the woodcocks, place them in the oven, and roast until they are cooked through, 30 to 35 minutes.

8. Remove the woodcocks from the oven, spread some of the Roasted Garlic over each one, and enjoy.

For the Stuffing

¾ cup unsalted butter

1 onion, diced

2 tablespoons chopped fresh parsley

2 garlic cloves, diced

8 slices of white bread, crusts removed, cut into 1-inch cubes

½ cup milk

1 egg

1 egg yolk

1 cup blueberries

Salt and pepper, to taste

For the Woodcock

4 woodcocks, plucked and gutted

2 tablespoons unsalted butter

Salt and pepper, to taste

1 tablespoon fresh thyme

Roasted Garlic
(see page 255)

Duck Jerky

2 lbs. boneless, skinless duck breasts

2 tablespoons brown sugar

2 tablespoons liquid smoke

¼ cup tamari or soy sauce

2 teaspoons kosher salt

1 teaspoon mushroom powder

1½ teaspoons black pepper

2 tablespoons Worcestershire sauce

2 teaspoons paprika

1. Trim any fat from the duck breasts and slice them into ¼-inch-thick strips.

2. Place the remaining ingredients in a mixing bowl and whisk until the sugar has dissolved and the mixture is thoroughly combined.

3. Add the meat to the marinade and stir until the strips are evenly coated.

4. Cover the bowl with plastic wrap, place it in the refrigerator, and let the duck marinate overnight.

5. Remove the meat from the refrigerator and give it a stir.

6. To prepare the jerky in a dehydrator, arrange the meat on the dehydrator trays, making sure to leave space between each piece. Place it in the dehydrator, set the temperature to 135°F, and dehydrate until the meat has dried out but is still flexible, 6 to 8 hours.

7. To prepare the jerky in an oven, preheat the oven to 150°F. Line two rimmed baking sheets with aluminum foil and place wire racks over the foil. Arrange the strips of meat on the racks, making sure to leave space between each piece and to keep the meat in a single layer. Place the pans in the oven and bake for 3 hours. Rotate the pans and then bake until the meat is dry to the touch, leathery, and slightly chewy, 2½ to 3½ hours.

8. Store the jerky at room temperature in an airtight container, where it will keep for a few weeks. If you are interested in a longer shelf life for your jerky, place it in a bag and vacuum seal it. Stored in a cool, dry place, the vacuum-sealed jerky will keep for 6 months to 2 years.

Duck Rillette

6 duck legs

Salt and pepper, to taste

2 tablespoons extra-virgin olive oil

¾ cup duck fat

½ cup fresh parsley, chopped

6 tablespoons unsalted butter, melted and cooled slightly

1. Pat the duck legs dry with paper towels and season them generously with salt and pepper. With the tip of a knife, gently poke the skin all around each leg. This will help release the fat as it renders. Let the legs rest at room temperature for at least 25 minutes.

2. Coat the bottom of a Dutch oven with the olive oil, add the duck legs, and set the oven to 285°F. Place the Dutch oven, uncovered, in the oven. You do not want to preheat the oven, as starting the duck at a low temperature allows its fat to render. After 1½ hours, check the duck. It should be under a layer of duck fat and the skin should be getting crisp. If the legs aren't browned and crispy, let the duck cook longer. When the skin is starting to crisp, raise the oven's temperature to 375°F and cook the duck for another 15 minutes.

3. Remove the pot from the oven, remove the duck legs from the fat, and let them rest for 10 minutes.

4. Remove the meat from the duck legs and finely chop it. Place the meat in a mixing bowl.

5. Add the duck fat and parsley, fold to combine, and season the mixture with salt and pepper.

6. Place the mixture in a jar, top it with the melted butter, and refrigerate until ready to serve. The rillette will keep in the refrigerator for 5 to 7 days.

Bacon-Wrapped Grouse

4 grouse breasts

1 teaspoon kosher salt

1 teaspoon black pepper

4 fresh sage leaves

4 strips of bacon

1 tablespoon extra-virgin olive oil

4 sprigs of fresh thyme

8 sprigs of fresh rosemary

2 apples, peeled, cores removed, cut into wedges

1. Preheat the oven to 350°F. Rinse the grouse breasts and pat them dry with paper towels.

2. Season the grouse with the salt and pepper, lay a sage leaf on top of each breast, and then wrap a slice of bacon tightly around each one, securing the bacon with toothpicks or skewers.

3. Place the olive oil in a large skillet and warm it over medium-high heat. Place the grouse in the skillet and sear it until the bacon is just starting to brown, turning the grouse as necessary.

4. Transfer the grouse to a baking dish and tuck a sprig of thyme and 2 sprigs of rosemary under the bacon. Add the apples to the baking dish, place it in the oven, and roast the grouse until it is cooked through, 20 to 25 minutes.

5. Remove the grouse from the oven and let it rest briefly before serving.

GAME BIRDS

Duck with Apple Lentils

For the Duck

1 duck, cleaned

¼ cup extra-virgin olive oil

Salt and pepper, to taste

6 shallots, sliced lengthways

2 celery stalks, chopped

2 large carrots, peeled and chopped

½ cup white wine

2 cups Chicken Stock (see page 253)

1 sprig of fresh parsley

For the Lentils

1 cup lentils

4 tablespoons unsalted butter

1 small onion, finely diced

1 apple, peeled, core removed, and diced

Juice of ½ lemon

Salt, to taste

1. Preheat the oven to 425°F. To begin preparations for the duck, rub the duck with a little bit of the olive oil, season it with salt and pepper, and place it in a deep baking dish.

2. Place the remaining olive oil in a large skillet and warm it over medium heat. Add the shallots and celery and cook, stirring occasionally, until they have softened, about 5 minutes. Stir in the carrots until they are coated and then transfer the vegetables to the baking dish.

3. Pour the white wine and stock into the baking dish, place the parsley sprig on top of the duck, and place it in the oven. Roast the duck for 20 minutes.

4. Baste the duck with the pan juices, lower the oven's temperature to 350°F, and roast the duck until it is cooked through, about 45 minutes.

5. While the duck is in the oven, begin preparations for the lentils. Bring a medium saucepan of water to a boil. Add the lentils and cook until they are tender but before they start to fall apart, about 25 minutes. Drain the lentils and set them aside.

6. Place the butter in a medium skillet and melt it over medium heat. Add the onion and cook, stirring occasionally, until it has softened, about 5 minutes. Stir in the apple, lemon juice, and lentils, season the mixture with salt, and cook for about 6 minutes.

7. Remove the duck from the oven and serve it alongside the lentils.

Bacon-Wrapped Pheasant

1¾ lb. young pheasant, plucked and gutted

Salt and pepper, to taste

2 tablespoons extra-virgin olive oil

6 strips of bacon

1 tablespoon unsalted butter

3 parsnips, peeled and quartered

3 onions, chopped

¾ cup white wine

4 sprigs of fresh thyme

1. Preheat the oven to 250°F. Season the pheasant, inside and out, with salt and pepper. Place the olive oil in a large skillet and warm it over medium heat. Place the pheasant in the pan and sear it until it is browned all over, turning it as necessary.

2. Place the pheasant in a roasting pan, breast side up, lay the bacon over the top, and place it in the oven. Roast the pheasant for 30 minutes.

3. While the pheasant is in the oven, place the butter in a large skillet and melt it over medium heat. Add the parsnips and onions and cook, stirring occasionally, until they are just starting to brown, about 6 minutes.

4. Remove the pheasant from the oven, add the parsnips, onions, wine, and thyme to the pan, and return the pan to the oven. Roast the pheasant until it is cooked through, another 1 to 1½ hours.

5. Remove the pheasant from the oven, carve it, and drizzle the pan juices over the top. Serve the pheasant alongside the vegetables.

Whole Guinea Fowl with Cranberry Sauce

4 tablespoons unsalted butter

1 onion, diced

1 red bell pepper, stem and seeds removed, sliced

2 bay leaves

Pinch of dried thyme

1¾ cups Chicken Stock (see page 253)

2 tablespoons cranberry sauce (see page 49)

1 guinea fowl, cleaned

Salt and pepper, to taste

1. Preheat the oven to 400°F. Place the butter in a Dutch oven and melt it over medium heat. Add the onion and bell pepper and cook, stirring occasionally, until they have softened, about 5 minutes.

2. Add the bay leaves, thyme, stock, and cranberry sauce and bring to a boil. Season the guinea fowl with salt and pepper, place it on top of the vegetables, and cover the pot.

3. Place the Dutch oven in the oven and cook for 45 minutes.

4. Remove the cover and cook until the guinea fowl is crispy and cooked through, about 20 minutes.

5. Remove the guinea fowl from the oven and enjoy.

Roast Duck

1 duck, cleaned

Salt and pepper, to taste

1 large onion, peeled and scored

1 large carrot, peeled and quartered lengthwise

4 sprigs of fresh rosemary

4 sprigs of fresh thyme

3 strips of bacon

1 cup dry red wine

1. Preheat the oven to 325°F. Rinse duck under cold water, pat the inside and out dry with paper towels, and season the duck with salt and pepper, including the cavity.

2. Place the onion and half of the carrots, rosemary, and thyme in the cavity of the duck. Lay the bacon strips lengthwise over the duck.

3. Place the duck in a roasting pan and arrange the remaining herbs and carrots around it. Pour the red wine over the duck and place it in the oven. Roast for 10 to 12 minutes per pound for rare, and 15 to 20 minutes per pound for well done. Baste the duck frequently while it roasts.

4. Remove the duck from the oven and let it rest for 10 minutes. Remove the vegetables and herbs from the cavity and discard the strips of bacon.

5. Transfer duck, herbs, and carrots to a serving platter and enjoy.

Winter Salad with Duck Breast

2 large beets

2 garlic cloves, minced

2 teaspoons flaxseeds

2 teaspoons whole-grain mustard

2 tablespoons fresh thyme, plus more for garnish

Salt and pepper, to taste

1 lb. boneless, skin-on duck breasts, trimmed

2 clementines, segmented

2 small heads of radicchio, leaves separated

¾ cup shelled walnuts

1 teaspoon Dijon mustard

1 tablespoon white wine vinegar

¼ cup extra-virgin olive oil

1. Preheat the oven to 375°F. Place the beets in a baking dish, add a few tablespoons of water, and cover the dish with aluminum foil. Place the beets in the oven and roast them until they are tender enough that a sharp knife inserted into them passes all the way to the center, about 1 hour. Remove the beets from the oven and let them cool. When they are cool enough to handle, peel and chop them. Set the beets aside.

2. Place the garlic, flaxseeds, whole-grain mustard, and thyme in a bowl, season the mixture with salt and pepper, and stir to combine.

3. Score the skins of the duck breasts in a cross-hatch pattern. Rub them with salt and pepper and place them in a large cast-iron skillet, skin side down. Place the pan over medium heat and cook until the fat has rendered. Pour the fat into a container and reserve it for another preparation. Turn the breasts over and remove their skins.

4. Spread the garlic-and-thyme mixture over the duck breasts, place the pan in the oven, and roast the duck breasts until they are cooked through, about 10 minutes.

5. Remove the roast duck from the oven, cover it loosely with aluminum foil, and let it rest for at least 10 minutes.

6. Place the clementines, radicchio, walnuts, and beets in a bowl and toss to combine.

7. Place the Dijon mustard and vinegar in a small bowl, season the mixture with salt and pepper, and whisk to combine. While whisking continually, add the olive oil in a slow, steady stream until it has emulsified.

8. Pour the dressing over the salad and toss to combine. Serve the sliced duck over the salads and garnish each portion with additional thyme.

Stuffed Quail

4 cups fresh bread crumbs

2 large eggs, beaten

2 small onions, chopped

2 garlic cloves, minced

Zest of 1 lemon

1 bunch of fresh parsley, chopped, plus more to taste

Salt and pepper, to taste

5 quail, cleaned

3 tablespoons extra-virgin olive oil

1. Preheat the oven to 400°F. Place the bread crumbs, eggs, onions, garlic, lemon zest, and parsley in a bowl, season the mixture with salt and pepper, and stir to combine.

2. Stuff the quail with the mixture. Truss the quail with kitchen twine and arrange them in a roasting pan. Brush the quail with the olive oil, season them with salt and pepper, and sprinkle additional parsley over the top.

3. Place the quail in the oven and roast them until the center of the stuffing registers at least 160°F, about 20 minutes.

4. Remove the quail from the oven and let them rest for 10 minutes before serving.

Peri-Peri Guinea Fowl

1 teaspoon coriander seeds

2 dried chiles, stems and seeds removed

1 tablespoon dried oregano

1 tablespoon sweet paprika

Pinch of cinnamon

2 teaspoons Worcestershire sauce

2 garlic cloves, minced

Juice of 1 lime

1 tablespoon honey

2 teaspoons kosher salt

5 tablespoons balsamic vinegar

1 tablespoon water

¼ cup extra-virgin olive oil

1 handful of fresh cilantro, roughly chopped

2 small guinea fowl, cleaned

Lime wedges, for serving

1. Place the coriander seeds and chiles in a small dry saucepan and toast them over medium heat for 1 minute, shaking the pan occasionally. Stir in the oregano, paprika, cinnamon, Worcestershire sauce, garlic, lime juice, honey, salt, balsamic vinegar, and water and bring the mixture to a simmer. Cook for about 10 minutes.

2. Transfer the mixture to a blender, add the olive oil and cilantro, and blitz until smooth. Let the sauce cool.

3. Truss the guinea fowl with kitchen twine. Rub half of the sauce over them, cover them, and let the guinea fowl marinate in the refrigerator overnight. Store the remaining sauce in the refrigerator.

4. Prepare a gas or charcoal grill for medium heat (about 400°F). Remove the guinea fowl from the marinade and place them on the grill. Cook the guinea fowl until they are cooked through, about 25 minutes, turning them regularly.

5. Brush the guinea fowl with the remaining sauce and serve with lime wedges.

Red Lentil Soup with Roasted Quail

3 tablespoons extra-virgin olive oil

1 large onion, chopped

2 large carrots, peeled and finely diced

Salt and pepper, to taste

2 garlic cloves, minced

1 tablespoon minced fresh ginger

2 teaspoons curry powder

1 teaspoon turmeric

1 cup split yellow lentils

4 cups Chicken Stock (see page 253)

4 boneless quail breasts, trimmed

1 teaspoon red pepper flakes

Fresh mint, for garnish

1. If using bamboo skewers, soak them in cold water for 30 minutes.

2. Place 2 tablespoons of the olive oil in a large saucepan and warm it over medium heat. Add the onion and carrots, season the vegetables with salt and pepper, and cook, stirring occasionally, until they have softened, about 5 minutes.

3. Add the garlic and ginger and cook, stirring continually, for 1 minute. Stir in the curry powder and turmeric and cook for another minute.

4. Add the lentils and stock and bring the soup to a boil. Reduce the heat and simmer the soup until the lentils are very tender, about 30 minutes.

5. Season the soup with salt and pepper and reduce the heat to the lowest possible setting to keep it warm.

6. Set the oven's broiler to high. Pat the quail breasts dry with paper towels, season them with salt and pepper, and sprinkle the red pepper flakes over the top. Cut the breasts in half and thread the pieces onto skewers.

7. Place the quail under the broiler and cook until they are browned and cooked through, 7 to 9 minutes, turning them as necessary. Remove the quail from the oven and let them rest for 5 minutes.

8. Ladle the soup into warmed bowls, top each portion with a skewer of quail, and garnish with mint.

Clementine-Stuffed Partridges

6 partridges, plucked and cleaned

Salt and pepper, to taste

2 bunches of fresh thyme

6 bay leaves

3 clementines, halved

2 tablespoons unsalted butter, softened

6 strips of bacon

1. Preheat the oven to 400°F. Rinse the partridges and pat them dry with paper towels. Season the cavities with salt and pepper and stuff them with the thyme, bay leaves, and clementines.

2. Arrange the partridges in a roasting pan and truss them with kitchen twine. Rub the butter all over their outsides and then wrap each partridge with a strip of bacon. Season them with pepper and place the pan in the oven.

3. Roast the partridges until the thickest part of the thighs registers at least 165°F, 30 to 35 minutes.

4. Remove the partridges from the oven and let them rest for 10 minutes before serving.

Roast Pheasant

2 small pheasants, cleaned

Salt and pepper, to taste

2 tablespoons extra-virgin olive oil

1 handful of fresh thyme

6 garlic cloves, minced

4 strips of bacon, halved crosswise

3 tablespoons unsalted butter, softened

2 small shallots, diced

4 cups wild mushrooms, chopped

¾ cup dry white wine

1 cup Chicken Stock (see page 253)

⅓ cup heavy cream

1. Preheat the oven to 350°F. Pat the pheasants dry with paper towels and season them inside and out with salt and pepper.

2. Place the olive oil in a large cast-iron skillet and warm it over medium heat. Add the pheasants and sear them until they are golden brown all over, turning them as necessary. Remove the pheasants from the pan and let them cool briefly.

3. Stuff the pheasants with the thyme and garlic and cover their breasts with the bacon.

4. Return the pheasants to the skillet and dot the pan with 1 tablespoon of butter. Place the skillet in the oven and roast the pheasants until they are cooked through, 30 to 40 minutes.

5. Remove the pheasants from the oven, transfer them to a platter, and loosely cover them with aluminum foil.

6. Place the remaining butter in the skillet and melt it over medium-low heat. Add the shallots and mushrooms, season them with salt, and cook, stirring occasionally, until the mushrooms are tender, 6 to 8 minutes.

7. Raise the heat to medium and deglaze the pan with the wine, scraping up any browned bits from the bottom of the pan. Cook until the wine has reduced by three-quarters, about 4 minutes.

8. Stir in the stock and bring the sauce to a boil. Cook until it has reduced by half, stir in the cream, and season the sauce with salt and pepper to taste. Bring the sauce to a simmer and cook until it just thickens, 1 to 2 minutes.

9. Serve the pheasants with the sauce on the side.

Guinea Fowl B'stilla

1. Place the olive oil in a Dutch oven and warm it over medium heat. Season the guinea fowl with salt, add it to the pot, and sear it until it is browned on both sides. Remove the guinea fowl from the pot and set it aside. Add the onions to the pot and cook, stirring occasionally, until they are golden, about 10 minutes.

2. Add the garlic and Ras el Hanout and cook, stirring continually, for 1 minute. Return the guinea fowl to the pot, add the water, and bring it to a boil. Reduce the heat, add the saffron, and cover the pot. Simmer the guinea fowl until the meat is tender and falls off the bones easily when pricked with a fork, about 40 minutes. Remove the guinea fowl from the pot and let it cool.

3. Bring the cooking liquid to a boil and cook it until it has reduced, about 15 minutes. Remove the pot from heat and let the liquid cool slightly. Add the cilantro and eggs and stir until most of the liquid has evaporated and the mixture has a dry, crumbly consistency. Let the mixture cool.

4. Preheat the oven to 350°F. Place the pine nuts in a dry skillet and toast them over high heat, shaking the pan occasionally, until they are golden brown. Transfer the toasted pine nuts to a bowl, add the sugar and orange blossom water, and stir until well combined. Set the mixture aside.

5. Shred the meat from the guinea fowl and season it with a little salt if necessary. Set it aside.

6. Brush a 9-inch pie plate generously with some of the butter. Fold each sheet of filo in half and brush each sheet with the melted butter. Keep the filo covered with a damp cloth while you assemble the pie.

7. Cover the base of the pie plate with 4 folded sheets of filo, so that it overhangs the sides.

8. Combine the guinea fowl, egg mixture, and pine nut mixture. Spread the mixture over the filo and cover it with 5 sheets of filo, brushing each sheet with more melted butter before placing it on top.

9. Fold the overhanging filo in toward the center of the pie. Cover the top with 3 more sheets of filo, brushing each sheet with melted butter. Tuck in the ends of the sheets on the edge and place the b'stilla in the oven.

10. Bake the b'stilla until it is golden brown on top, about 30 minutes. Remove it from the oven, sprinkle cinnamon and confectioners' sugar over it, and enjoy.

2 tablespoons extra-virgin olive oil

2 lbs. guinea fowl, cleaned

Salt, to taste

2 onions, finely diced

4 garlic cloves, minced

1 tablespoon Ras el Hanout (see page 257)

1¾ cups water

2 pinches of saffron

¼ cup chopped fresh cilantro

5 eggs

¼ cup pine nuts

¼ cup sugar

2 tablespoons orange blossom water

10 tablespoons unsalted butter, melted

10½ oz. frozen filo dough, thawed

Cinnamon, for dusting

Confectioners' sugar, for dusting

Quail with Prosciutto & Artichokes

4 quail, cleaned

Salt and pepper, to taste

2 tablespoons extra-virgin olive oil

2 tablespoons unsalted butter

1 lemon, sliced

1 handful of fresh thyme

8 slices of prosciutto

1 tablespoon fresh lemon juice

8 artichoke hearts

Pear & Cranberry Chutney (see page 276), for serving

1. Preheat the oven to 425°F. Season the quail inside and out with salt and pepper. Place the olive oil and butter in a roasting pan and warm the mixture over medium heat. Add the quail and sear them until they are browned all over, turning them as necessary.

2. Remove the quail from the pan and stuff them with the lemon slices and thyme. Wrap two slices of prosciutto around each quail, place them in the oven, and roast them until they are cooked through and the prosciutto is crispy, 15 to 20 minutes.

3. Bring salted water to a boil in a saucepan. Add the lemon juice and artichokes and cook until the artichokes are tender, about 20 minutes. Drain the artichokes and set them aside.

4. Remove the quail from the oven and serve them alongside the artichokes and chutney.

Pheasant Forestiere

1½ lb. pheasant, cleaned

½ cup unsalted butter

Salt and pepper, to taste

1 tablespoon juniper berries

4 strips of bacon, 2 left
whole; 2 finely diced

2½ cups mushrooms

Fresh rosemary, chopped,
for garnish

Fresh mint, chopped,
for garnish

1. Preheat the oven to 400°F. Rub half of the butter over the pheasant and season it generously with salt and pepper. Place the pheasant in a roasting pan and spoon some of the juniper berries into the pheasant's cavity. Sprinkle the rest on top.

2. Place the pheasant in the oven and roast it until the interior is 165°F and the juices run clear when the thickest part of a thigh is pierced, about 1 hour.

3. Remove the pheasant from the oven and cover it loosely with aluminum foil.

4. Set the oven's broiler to high, place the whole strips of bacon on a baking sheet, place them in the oven, and broil the bacon until it is golden brown and crispy, 2 to 4 minutes, turning the bacon as necessary.

5. Place the remaining butter in a large skillet and melt it over medium heat. Add the mushrooms and finely diced bacon and cook, stirring occasionally, until they are browned, 8 to 10 minutes.

6. Place the mushrooms and bacon in a serving dish and rest the pheasant on top. Garnish the dish with the rosemary and mint and enjoy.

Pheasant in Salt & Herb Crust

1 cup kosher salt

½ cup all-purpose flour, plus more as needed

1 tablespoon dried rosemary

1 tablespoon dried sage

1 tablespoon dried thyme

1 teaspoon ground juniper berries

1 cup ice water

1½ lb. pheasant, cleaned

Fresh thyme, for garnish

1. Place the salt, flour, rosemary, sage, dried thyme, and juniper berries in a mixing bowl and stir to combine. Pour in the ice water and stir the mixture with a wooden spoon until it comes together as a rough dough.

2. Knead the dough by hand until it is a smooth ball. Cover the bowl with plastic wrap and chill it in the refrigerator for 1 hour.

3. Preheat the oven to 450°F. Line a baking sheet with parchment paper. Place the dough on a flour-dusted work surface and roll it into a ¼-inch-thick oval. Lay the dough over the breast of the pheasant and wrap it around the bird, molding it to the pheasant's shape. Pinch the seam to seal the pheasant, place it on the baking sheet, and place it in the oven.

4. Bake the pheasant until the internal temperature reaches 165°F, 45 to 50 minutes. Remove the pheasant from the oven and let it rest for 10 minutes.

5. Remove the salt crust, carve the pheasant, and garnish each serving with fresh thyme.

Roasted Game Hens

½ cup kosher salt, plus more to taste

12 cups cold water

4 game hens

6 tablespoons unsalted butter, softened

1 tablespoon chopped fresh sage

1 tablespoon fresh thyme

2 teaspoons chopped fresh rosemary

2 teaspoons black pepper, plus more to taste

3 tablespoons all-purpose flour

¼ cup dry white wine

2½ cups Chicken Stock (see page 253)

2 cups fresh spinach

1 cup fresh parsley

1. Place the salt and water in a large stockpot and stir until the salt has dissolved. Add the game hens, cover the pot, and chill it in the refrigerator for 2 hours.

2. Preheat the oven to 400°F. Remove the game hens from the brine, rinse them thoroughly, and pat them dry with paper towels. Prick their skins all over with a fork or a paring knife.

3. Preheat oven to 400°F. Place the butter, sage, thyme, 1 teaspoon of rosemary, and pepper in a bowl, season the mixture with salt, and stir to combine. Set the mixture aside.

4. Place the game hens, breast side down, on a wire rack set in a rimmed baking sheet. Place them in the oven and roast until they are golden brown, about 20 minutes.

5. Remove the game hens from the oven and spread 1 teaspoon of the herb butter over the back of each one. Turn the game hens over and spread 2 teaspoons herb butter over their breasts and legs.

6. Return the game hens to the oven, pour 1 cup of water in the baking sheet, and roast the game hens for another 20 minutes.

7. Remove the game hens from the oven and spread the remaining herb butter over them. Return them to the oven and pour another ½ cup of water into the baking sheet. Raise the oven's temperature to 450°F and roast the game hens until their internal temperate is 165°F, about 20 minutes. Remove them from the oven and let them rest for 5 minutes.

8. Place the spinach, parsley, and remaining rosemary in a mixing bowl, season the mixture with salt and pepper, and toss to combine.

9. To serve, place the game hens on a bed of the spinach-and-herb mixture.

Wild Goose with Apple & Chestnut Stuffing

¾ cup heavy cream

1 large egg

1 teaspoon dried sage

1 teaspoon dried parsley

1 teaspoon dried thyme

Salt and pepper, to taste

1 cup day-old bread cubes, toasted

2 tablespoons extra-virgin olive oil

1 small onion, finely chopped

1 large apple, peeled, core removed, cut into ½-inch cubes

½ cup quartered chestnuts

½ cup pitted prunes

8 lb. goose, cleaned

1 lemon, halved

½ cup corn syrup

½ cup unsalted butter, melted

¼ cup brandy

1. Place the cream, egg, sage, parsley, and thyme in a mixing bowl, season the mixture with salt and pepper, and stir to combine. Add the bread cubes and stir to combine. Cover the bowl and refrigerate until the bread has absorbed all of the liquid, at least 3 hours.

2. Preheat the oven to 350°F. Remove the soaked bread from the refrigerator.

3. Place the olive oil in a large skillet and warm it over medium-high heat. Add the onion and cook, stirring occasionally, until it has softened, about 5 minutes. Add the apple, chestnuts, and prunes and cook, stirring occasionally, until the flavors are blended, about 6 minutes. Remove the pan from heat and stir the mixture into the soaked bread.

4. Rinse the goose under cold water and pat it dry with paper towels. Remove any excess skin flaps or noticeable pockets of fat. Prick the skin liberally with a fork. Rub the lemon halves inside the cavity and then stuff the goose with the stuffing. Truss the goose with kitchen twine and place it in a roasting pan.

5. Place the corn syrup, butter, and brandy in a bowl and whisk to combine. Brush the outside of the goose liberally with the syrup.

6. Place the goose in the oven and roast it until the internal temperature reaches 165°F, about 3 hours, basting it every half hour with syrup.

7. Remove the goose from the oven and let it rest for 15 minutes before carving.

GAME BIRDS

153

Pheasant with Roasted Fruit Medley

1 cup cherries

1 small apple, core removed, diced

1 plum, pit removed, diced

1 large shallot, sliced

1 tablespoon balsamic vinegar

¼ cup extra-virgin olive oil

1 pheasant, cleaned and split in half lengthwise

2 teaspoons kosher salt

Fresh chervil, for garnish

1. Preheat the oven to 350°F. Line a baking sheet with parchment paper. Place the fruit and shallot in a mixing bowl, drizzle the vinegar and half of the olive oil over the mixture, and stir to combine. Transfer the fruit mixture to the baking sheet, place it in the oven, and roast until it starts to caramelize, about 25 minutes.

2. While the fruit is in the oven, place the remaining olive oil in a large cast-iron skillet and warm it over medium-high heat. Season the pheasant with the salt and add to the pan, breast side down. Cook the pheasant for 6 minutes, turn it over, and cook another 6 minutes.

3. Place the skillet in the oven and cook the pheasant until the internal temperature is 145°F.

4. Remove the pheasant and roasted fruit from the oven. Top the pheasant with the roasted fruit and garnish the dish with fresh chervil.

WILD BOAR

As anyone who has spent considerable time out in the woods will tell you, a boar is a fearsome foe. But, should one manage to best one, there is a considerable reward—a rich flavor that is capable of working in a number of decadent dishes.

Arrosto di Cinghiale

2 lb. boneless leg of wild boar, trimmed

Salt and pepper, to taste

2 onions, chopped

2 carrots, peeled and chopped

¼ celeriac, peeled and chopped

5 bay leaves

2 cups red wine

3 tablespoons white wine vinegar

5 tablespoons extra-virgin olive oil

1½ cups Roasted Chestnuts (see page 258)

2 tablespoons chopped fresh rosemary

4 garlic cloves, crushed

1 tablespoon honey

1. Pat the boar dry with paper towels and season it with salt and pepper. Place the boar in a deep roasting pan and arrange the onions, carrots, celeriac, and bay leaves around it. Pour the red wine and white wine vinegar over the boar, cover the roasting pan with aluminum foil, and let the boar marinate in the refrigerator for 2 days, turning it over occasionally.

2. Preheat the oven to 300°F. Remove the boar from the marinade (reserving the marinade) and pat it dry with paper towels. Place the olive oil in a large skillet and warm it over medium heat. Add the boar to the pan and sear it until it is browned all over, turning it as necessary. Place the boar in a clean roasting pan.

3. Strain the marinade and add ½ cup to the roasting pan containing the boar. Arrange the chestnuts around the boar, add the rosemary and garlic, and place the pan on the lowest rack in the oven. Roast the boar until it is tender, about 1½ hours, basting occasionally.

4. Remove the pan from the oven, cover it loosely with aluminum foil, and let the boar rest for about 10 minutes.

5. Stir the honey into the pan juices. Slice the boar into thin slices and serve it alongside the chestnuts and pan juices.

WILD BOAR

159

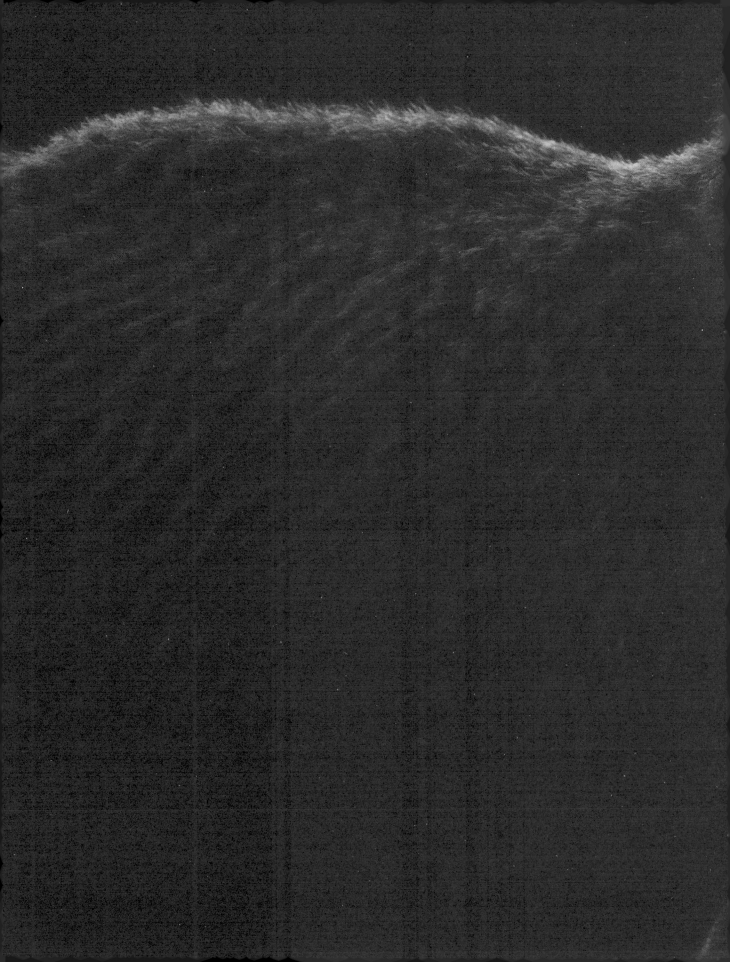

Wild Boar Stew with Cabbage

1. To begin preparations for the stew, place the bacon in a medium saucepan and cook it over medium heat, stirring occasionally, until it is crispy, about 8 minutes. Remove the bacon with a slotted spoon and transfer it to a paper towel–lined plate.

2. Add the olive oil to the pan and warm it over medium heat. Season the boar with salt, pepper, and the paprika. Working in batches to avoid crowding the pan, add the boar and cook until it is browned all over, turning it as necessary. Remove the boar from the pan and set it aside.

3. Add the onions to the pan and cook, stirring occasionally, until they are translucent, about 3 minutes. Add the garlic and tomato paste and cook, stirring continually, for 1 minute.

4. Deglaze the pan with half of the beer, scraping up any browned bits from the bottom of the pan. Return the boar and bacon to the pan, add the stock and the remaining beer, and bring the stew to a simmer.

5. Add the remaining ingredients, except for the mashed potatoes, and cook the boar until it is very tender, 1½ to 2 hours.

6. While the stew is simmering, prepare the cabbage. Place the butter in a large skillet and melt it over medium heat. Add the sugar, cook for 1 minute, and then add the onion and apples. Cook, stirring, until they have softened, about 5 minutes. Add the remaining ingredients and cook until the cabbage is tender, about 45 minutes, adding water to the pan if it starts to look dry.

7. Remove the bay leaves from the stew and discard them. Ladle the stew into warmed bowls and serve alongside the cabbage and mashed potatoes.

For the Stew

4 strips of bacon, finely diced

2 tablespoons extra-virgin olive oil

2 lbs. wild boar shoulder, trimmed and cubed

Salt and pepper, to taste

2 pinches of paprika

14 oz. onions, finely diced

2 garlic cloves, finely diced

1 tablespoon tomato paste

1¼ cups lager

1 cup Beef Stock (see page 250)

2 bay leaves

½ teaspoon juniper berries, ground

1 teaspoon chopped fresh rosemary

2 teaspoons fresh thyme

Mashed potatoes (see page 68), for serving

For the Cabbage

2½ tablespoons Clarified Butter (see page 256)

1 tablespoon sugar

1 onion, finely diced

2 apples, peeled, cores removed, finely diced

10 cups thinly sliced red cabbage

¼ cup white vinegar

Salt, to taste

2 bay leaves

3 whole cloves

1 cup Beef Stock (see page 250)

Wild Boar with Dumplings

2½ lb. boneless wild boar shoulder

4 whole cloves

2 onions

1 celery stalk, chopped

1 carrot, peeled and chopped

3 cups dry red wine

6 tablespoons white wine vinegar

1 bay leaf

1 teaspoon peppercorns

1 teaspoon juniper berries

¼ cup Clarified Butter (see page 256)

1½ cups Beef Stock (see page 250)

Salt and pepper, to taste

Pinch of sugar

1 tablespoon cornstarch

1 tablespoon water

Classic Dumplings (see page 268)

1. Place the boar in a large bowl and set it aside. Stick the cloves into the onions and add them to a pot with the celery, carrot, red wine, vinegar, bay leaf, peppercorns, and juniper berries. Bring the brine to a boil, remove it from heat, and let it cool completely.

2. Pour the brine over the meat, cover the bowl, and chill it in the refrigerator for 3 days, turning the boar from time to time.

3. Preheat the oven to 350°F. Remove the boar from the brine, reserve the brine, and pat the boar dry. Place the butter in a Dutch oven and warm it over medium-high heat. Add the boar to the pot and sear it until it is browned all over, turning it as necessary.

4. Deglaze the pot with some of the stock, scraping up any browned bits from the bottom of the pan, bring it to a simmer, and braise the boar until it is fork-tender, about 2 hours, adding some of the reserved brine and the remaining stock as necessary.

5. Remove the boar from the pot and let it rest for 10 minutes.

6. Season the sauce with salt and pepper and stir in the sugar. Whisk the cornstarch and water together in a small bowl and then stir the slurry into the sauce. Bring the sauce to a boil and cook until it has thickened slightly.

7. To cook the dumplings, either drop them into the simmering sauce or pan-fry them and serve them alongside the boar and the sauce.

165

Wild Boar Terrine

1 teaspoon black peppercorns

5 juniper berries

Pinch of freshly grated nutmeg

½ teaspoon dried marjoram

½ teaspoon dried thyme

2 teaspoons kosher salt

4 teaspoons Cognac

4 teaspoons Port

1¾ lbs. wild boar, trimmed and diced

½ lb. bacon, diced

1 onion, diced

2 eggs, beaten

5 oz. smoked pork belly, finely diced

1. Use a mortar and pestle to grind the peppercorns and juniper berries. Place them in a bowl, add the nutmeg, marjoram, thyme, salt, Cognac, and Port and stir to combine. Add the boar and bacon to the marinade, cover the bowl, and let the mixture marinate in the refrigerator overnight.

2. Preheat the oven to 350°F. Add the onion to the mixture and grind it finely with a food processor. Add the eggs and pork belly to the mixture and stir until well incorporated.

3. Transfer the meat mixture to ovenproof jars and place the jars in a deep roasting pan. Pour boiling water into the pan until the water reaches halfway up the jars. Place the pan in the oven and bake until the terrines are set, about 1 hour.

4. Remove the pan from the oven, remove the terrines from the pan, and let them cool completely before serving.

Wild Boar Burgers with Blueberry Mayonnaise

1 cup mayonnaise

¼ cup blueberry jam

1 lb. ground wild boar

½ lb. ground sausage

Salt and pepper, to taste

1 tablespoon extra-virgin olive oil

4 tablespoons unsalted butter

1 leek, trimmed, rinsed well, and sliced

1 pear, core removed, sliced

4 hamburger buns

8 slices of bacon, cooked

1. Place the mayonnaise and blueberry jam in a small bowl and stir until well combined. Set the mayonnaise aside.

2. Place the boar and sausage in a bowl, season the mixture with salt and pepper, and work the mixture with your hands until combined. Form the mixture into 4 patties.

3. Place the olive oil in a large skillet and warm it over medium-high heat. Add the burgers to the pan and cook until they are cooked through, 12 to 15 minutes, turning them halfway through.

4. While the burgers are cooking, place the butter in a large skillet and melt it over medium-high heat. Add the leek and cook, stirring occasionally, until it has softened, about 8 minutes.

5. Reduce the heat to medium, push the leek to the side of the pan, and add the pear. Cook the pear until it is caramelized on each side, about 2 minutes per side.

6. Assemble the burgers with the buns, blueberry mayo, pear-and-leek mixture, and bacon and enjoy.

Roast Wild Boar with Red Cabbage & Mushrooms

1. To begin preparations for the boar, pat the boar dry with paper towels and place it on a baking sheet. Rub the peppercorns and salt into the meat and place it in the refrigerator for 24 hours.

2. Remove the boar from the refrigerator and let it rest at room temperature for 1 hour. Preheat the oven to 400°F.

3. Place the boar on a rack set inside a large roasting pan and drizzle the olive oil over it. Press the rosemary into the boar, place it in the oven, and roast it until the thickest part registers 140°F, 2 to 2½ hours.

4. While the boar is in the oven, prepare the cabbage. Place the butter in a large skillet and melt it over medium heat. Add the cinnamon stick, cloves, juniper berries, and cabbage, cook for 1 minute, and then add the remaining ingredients. Cover the pan, reduce the heat to low, and cook until the cabbage is very tender, about 1 hour, stirring occasionally.

5. Remove the boar from the oven, cover it loosely with aluminum foil, and let it rest for 20 minutes.

6. To prepare the mushrooms, place the olive oil and butter in a large skillet and warm the mixture over medium heat. Add the shallot and mushrooms, season the vegetables with salt, and cook, stirring occasionally, until the mushrooms are browned, about 10 minutes.

7. Garnish the roast boar with rosemary and serve it alongside the cabbage, mushrooms, and mashed potatoes.

For the Boar

5 lb. leg of wild boar, trimmed

3 tablespoons black peppercorns, crushed

3 tablespoons kosher salt

3 tablespoons extra-virgin olive oil

1 tablespoon chopped fresh rosemary

Fresh rosemary, for garnish

Mashed potatoes (see page 68), for serving

For the Cabbage

2 tablespoons unsalted butter

1 cinnamon stick

1 teaspoon whole cloves

¾ teaspoon juniper berries

1 large head of red cabbage, shredded

¾ cup brown sugar

½ cup red wine vinegar

1 cup red wine

For the Mushrooms

1 tablespoon extra-virgin olive oil

2 tablespoons unsalted butter

½ shallot, finely diced

3 cups chanterelle mushrooms

Salt, to taste

Slow-Cooked BBQ Boar Sliders

3½ lb. wild boar shoulder

Salt and pepper, to taste

2¼ cups BBQ Sauce (see page 259)

1 cup water

12 slider buns

1. Pat the boar dry with paper towels, cut it into two pieces, and season it generously with salt and pepper. Place it in a slow cooker.

2. Pour the BBQ Sauce and water over the boar, cover the slow cooker, and cook the boar on low for 8 hours, turning the meat over halfway through.

3. Transfer the wild boar to a cutting board and let it cool slightly. Using 2 forks, shred the meat.

4. Assemble the sliders with the boar and slider buns and enjoy.

Garlic & Soy Wild Boar

2 lbs. wild boar shoulder, trimmed and cubed

3 garlic cloves, chopped

1 cup soy sauce

1 cup white vinegar

1 bay leaf

1 teaspoon black peppercorns, crushed

1 cup water

1 tablespoon brown sugar

2 tablespoons extra-virgin olive oil

1. Place the boar in a container with a tight-fitting lid. Add the remaining ingredients, except for the olive oil, and stir to combine. Cover the container and let the boar marinate in the refrigerator overnight.

2. Remove the boar from the marinade, reserve the marinade, and pat the boar dry. Place the olive oil in a Dutch oven and warm it over medium-high heat. Add the boar and sear it until it is browned all over, turning it as necessary.

3. Pour the marinade into the pot and bring it to a boil. Reduce the heat to low, cover the pot, and simmer the boar until it is very tender, about 1 hour.

4. Serve the boar immediately.

Wild Boar Spareribs

¾ cup brown sugar

1 tablespoon paprika

1 tablespoon garlic powder

1 teaspoon kosher salt

1 teaspoon black pepper

¼ teaspoon cayenne pepper

2 racks of wild boar spareribs, halved

2 cups BBQ Sauce
(see page 259)

1. Preheat the oven to 300°F. Place the brown sugar, paprika, garlic powder, salt, black pepper, and cayenne in a small bowl and stir to combine.

2. Place the spareribs on a cutting board and remove the thin membrane that is on the bone side of the ribs. Lay out four sheets of aluminum foil and place a half rack on top of each. Massage each side of the spareribs with about 1 tablespoon of the dry rub. Cover the ribs with another sheet of foil and fold the edges over to seal the packets tightly. Place the spareribs in the oven and bake them for 2 hours.

3. Remove the ribs from the oven. Line a baking sheet with aluminum foil. Set the oven's broiler on high. Carefully unwrap the ribs and transfer them to the foil-lined baking sheet. Brush them with the BBQ Sauce and place them under the broiler. Broil until the BBQ Sauce begins to caramelize, about 8 minutes.

4. Remove the ribs from the oven, slice them, and enjoy.

Wild Boar & Chestnut Ragout with Spätzle

2 tablespoons avocado oil

1 lb. wild boar, trimmed and cubed

Salt and pepper, to taste

1 large onion, diced

¼ cup diced bacon

¼ cup diced green bell pepper

¼ cup diced red bell pepper

¼ cup diced yellow bell pepper

¼ cup chopped Roasted Chestnuts (see page 258)

2 tablespoons tomato paste

¼ cup soy sauce

½ cup red wine

1 cup water

2 juniper berries

2 whole cloves

1 lb. green beans, trimmed

Spätzle (see page 260)

1. Place the avocado oil in a large skillet and warm it over medium-high heat. Season the boar with salt and pepper, add it to the pan, and sear it until it is browned all over.

2. Add the bacon, onion, bell peppers, and chestnuts and cook, stirring, until the vegetables and bacon start to brown, about 8 minutes.

3. Stir in the tomato paste, soy sauce, wine, juniper berries, and cloves, season the sauce with salt and pepper, and bring it to a simmer. Reduce the heat to low, cover the pan, and cook until the boar is very tender, about 2 hours, stirring occasionally.

4. Bring salted water to a boil in a large saucepan. Add the green beans and cook until they are tender, 2 to 3 minutes.

5. Drain the green beans. Stir the Spätzle into the sauce and cook until they are warmed through. Serve the Spätzle alongside the green beans and enjoy.

Wild Boar with Chanterelles

2 lb. wild boar tenderloin

Salt and pepper, to taste

2 tablespoons avocado oil

½ cup unsalted butter, sliced

2 tablespoons all-purpose flour

1 cup Mushroom Stock (see page 254)

1 lb. chanterelle mushrooms

Fresh thyme, for garnish

1. Preheat the oven to 400°F. Season the wild boar with salt and pepper.

2. Place the avocado oil in a large cast-iron skillet and warm it over medium-high heat. Add the wild boar and sear it until it is browned all over, turning it as necessary.

3. Turn off the heat and place half of butter on top of the wild boar. Place the pan in the oven and roast the wild boar until the internal temperature is 140°F, 15 to 20 minutes.

4. Remove the wild boar from the oven, transfer it to a cutting board, and let it rest for 10 minutes.

5. Place 2 tablespoons of the pan drippings in a medium saucepan and warm them over medium heat. Add the flour and whisk until it has been absorbed. Add the stock and bring the gravy to a boil. Reduce the heat to medium-low and simmer the gravy until it has the desired consistency.

6. Place the remaining butter in a clean large skillet and melt it over medium-high heat. Add the mushrooms and cook until they are just starting to caramelize, about 10 minutes, stirring once or twice.

7. To serve, slice the wild boar, top each portion with some of the gravy and mushrooms, and garnish with thyme.

Polenta with Wild Boar Stew

2 cups red wine

1 vanilla bean pod, halved lengthwise

¼ teaspoon whole cloves

1 cinnamon stick

2 lbs. wild boar shoulder, trimmed and cubed

2 tablespoons extra-virgin olive oil

1 onion, diced

2 carrots, peeled and diced

1 celery stalk, diced

Salt and pepper, to taste

1 teaspoon herbes de Provence

1 tablespoon tomato paste

1 cup Beef Stock (see page 250)

4 tablespoons unsalted butter

6 cups water

1 cup medium-grain cornmeal

Fresh rosemary, chopped, for garnish

Fresh thyme, for garnish

1. Place the wine, vanilla bean pod, cloves, and cinnamon stick in a medium saucepan and bring the mixture to a boil. Remove the pan from heat and let the brine cool to room temperature.

2. Place the wild boar in a container with a tight-fitting lid. Pour the brine over it, cover the container, and let the boar marinate in the refrigerator overnight.

3. Place the olive oil in a Dutch oven and warm it over medium-high heat. Add the onion, carrots, and celery and cook, stirring occasionally, until they have softened, about 10 minutes.

4. Remove the boar from the brine, reserve the brine, add the boar to the Dutch oven, season it with salt and pepper, and sear it until it is browned all over, turning it as necessary.

5. Add the brine, herbes de Provence, and tomato paste and bring the stew to a boil. Reduce the heat to medium-low, cover the pot, and cook the stew until the boar it is very tender, about 2 hours, stirring occasionally. Add the stock as necessary to keep the boar covered with liquid.

6. Place the butter in a saucepan and melt it over medium heat. Add the water and bring to a boil. Gradually add the cornmeal, whisking continually to prevent lumps from forming. When all of the cornmeal has been incorporated, reduce the heat to low and cook, stirring for 1 minute for every 10 minutes of cooking time, until the polenta is creamy, about 40 minutes.

7. Season the polenta with salt, ladle it into warmed bowls, and top each portion with some of the stew. Garnish with rosemary and thyme and enjoy.

Spicy Wild Boar Chops

2 zucchini, halved lengthwise and sliced

1 cup grape tomatoes

2 tablespoons extra-virgin olive oil

1 tablespoon balsamic vinegar

Salt, to taste

4 wild boar chops

1½ teaspoons garlic powder

1 tablespoon avocado oil

1 teaspoon cayenne pepper

1 teaspoon paprika

½ teaspoon white peppercorns, crushed

Crusty bread, toasted, for serving

Apricot Jam (see page 261), for serving

1. Preheat the oven to 400°F. Place the zucchini and tomatoes in a bowl, add the olive oil and vinegar, and season the mixture with salt. Toss to combine and spread the vegetables on a baking sheet in an even layer.

2. Place the vegetables in the oven and roast until they are tender and starting to brown, about 30 minutes.

3. While the vegetables are in the oven, season the boar chops with salt and the garlic powder.

4. Place the avocado oil in a large cast-iron skillet and warm it over medium-high heat. Add the boar chops and sear them until browned on each side, turning them as necessary.

5. Place the pan in the oven and roast the boar chops until they are cooked through, about 10 minutes.

6. Remove the boar chops and the vegetables from the oven and let them rest.

7. Place the cayenne, paprika, and peppercorns in a small bowl and stir to combine.

8. Place the roasted vegetables in a serving dish, top with the boar chops, and then sprinkle the cayenne mixture over the top. Serve with crusty bread and Apricot Jam and enjoy.

RABBIT

Rabbit is not only delicious, it is also plentiful. These recipes will encourage you to do the responsible thing: making a hunting excursion centered around rabbits a regular occurrence.

Larded Saddle of Rabbit

1 teaspoon kosher salt

¼ teaspoon cinnamon

¼ teaspoon ground ginger

Zest of ½ lemon

1 saddle of rabbit
(about 2 lbs.)

½ lb. bacon, strips cut in half
lengthwise

1 tablespoon extra-virgin
olive oil

4 tablespoons unsalted butter

1 cup dry red wine

2½ cups fresh porcini
mushrooms, sliced

2 shallots, diced

Black pepper, to taste

1. Place the salt, cinnamon, ginger, and lemon zest in a bowl and stir to combine. Rub the mixture onto the rabbit, cover it in plastic wrap, and refrigerate the rabbit for 2 hours.

2. Preheat the oven to 400°F. Using a larding needle, push the strips of bacon roughly ¼ inch under the surface of the rabbit, equally spaced, so that the ends of the bacon protrude from the meat by approximately ¼ inch.

3. Place the olive oil and butter in a roasting pan and warm the mixture over medium heat. Add the rabbit and sear it until it is browned all over, turning it as necessary. Pour the red wine into the pan and bring it to a boil.

4. Transfer the rabbit to the oven and roast for 5 minutes. Add the mushrooms and shallots, baste the rabbit, and roast it until it is cooked through, about 15 minutes.

5. Remove the rabbit from the oven, season it with pepper, and enjoy.

Braised Rabbit with Tomatoes

4 garlic cloves, minced

6 tablespoons extra-virgin olive oil

Salt and pepper, to taste

1 tablespoon chopped fresh tarragon

3¼ lb. rabbit, cut into 8 pieces

1 onion, sliced

¾ cup dry white wine

12 cherry tomatoes

Fresh parsley, chopped, for garnish

Fresh sage, chopped, for garnish

1. Place the garlic, ¼ cup of olive oil, pepper, and tarragon in a bowl and stir to combine. Brush the mixture onto the rabbit.

2. Place the remaining olive oil in a roasting pan and warm it over medium heat. Add the rabbit and sear it until it is browned all over, about 15 minutes, turning it as necessary.

3. Stir in the onion and wine. Cover the roasting pan and braise the rabbit for 25 minutes.

4. Stir in the tomatoes, cover the pan, and braise the rabbit until it is cooked through and tender, about 15 minutes.

5. Season the dish with salt and pepper, garnish it with parsley and sage, and enjoy.

Rabbit with Tapenade

2 saddles of rabbit
(about 4½ lbs.)

Salt and pepper, to taste

2 tablespoons all-purpose
flour

2 tablespoons unsalted butter

¼ cup Tapenade
(see page 264)

4 sprigs of fresh rosemary

8 strips of bacon

Arugula, for garnish

1. Preheat the oven to 350°F. Divide each saddle of rabbit into 2 pieces, season them with salt and pepper, and coat them lightly with the flour.

2. Coat a roasting pan with the butter. Rub about 1 tablespoon of Tapenade on each piece of meat. Place a sprig of rosemary on each piece, wrap them with the bacon, and tie closed with kitchen twine.

3. Place the rabbit in the roasting pan, place it in the oven, and roast the rabbit until it is cooked through and tender, about 35 minutes, turning the meat twice during cooking.

4. Remove the rabbit from the oven, garnish it with arugula, and enjoy.

RABBIT

Braised Rabbit with Artichokes, Shallots & Tomatoes

2 tablespoons extra-virgin olive oil

8 shallots, quartered

2 garlic cloves, minced

3 lb. rabbit, cut into 8 pieces

Salt and pepper, to taste

¼ cup dry white wine

1⅔ cups Chicken Stock (see page 253)

1 teaspoon fresh thyme, plus more for garnish

1 tablespoon chopped fresh rosemary, plus more for garnish

6 artichoke hearts

4 Roma tomatoes, halved lengthwise

1. Place the olive oil in a Dutch oven and warm it over medium heat. Add the shallots and cook, stirring occasionally, until they have softened, about 5 minutes.

2. Add the garlic and cook, stirring continually, for 1 minute. Remove the mixture from the pan and set it aside.

3. Season the rabbit with salt and pepper, add it to the pot, and sear it until it is browned all over, 10 to 15 minutes, turning the rabbit as necessary.

4. Add the wine, raise the heat to high, and bring it to a boil, scraping up any browned bits from the bottom. Cook until the wine has reduced by one-third.

5. Add the stock, return the shallots and garlic to the pot, and add the thyme and rosemary. Reduce the heat to low, cover the Dutch oven, and braise the rabbit for 40 minutes.

6. Add the artichoke hearts and tomatoes and cook until the rabbit is very tender, about 20 minutes.

7. Remove the rabbit and vegetables from the pot and transfer them to a serving dish. Place the Dutch oven over high heat and cook the sauce until it has reduced and thickened slightly.

8. Spoon the sauce over the rabbit and vegetables, garnish the dish with additional thyme and rosemary, and enjoy.

Rabbit & Sausage Crostini

3 tablespoons extra-virgin olive oil

1 small onion, finely diced

1 celery stalk, finely diced

2 garlic cloves, minced

1 teaspoon fennel seeds

½ lb. ground hot Italian sausage

½ lb. rabbit, minced

2 cups diced tomatoes

½ cup dry red wine

Salt and pepper, to taste

1 Baguette (see page 262), cut into 12 slices

Fresh rosemary, for garnish

1. Preheat the oven to 350°F. Place 1 tablespoon of olive oil in a large skillet and warm it over medium-high heat. Add the onion and celery and cook, stirring occasionally, until the onion is translucent, about 3 minutes. Stir in the garlic and fennel seeds and cook, stirring continually, for 1 minute.

2. Add the sausage and rabbit to the pan and cook, stirring occasionally, until they have browned, about 6 minutes.

3. Drain any excess fat from the pan, stir in the tomatoes and red wine, and season the dish with salt and pepper. Cover the pan and simmer the mixture until the sausage and rabbit are cooked through and the liquid has nearly evaporated, 15 to 20 minutes.

4. Lightly brush the bread with the remaining olive oil and place them on a baking sheet. Place the bread in the oven and bake until it is crispy and golden brown, 10 to 15 minutes.

5. Remove the bread from the oven, spoon the rabbit-and-sausage mixture over the slices, garnish with rosemary, and enjoy.

Rabbit Stifado

¼ cup extra-virgin olive oil

3¼ lb. rabbit, cut into 8 pieces

Salt and pepper, to taste

2 celery stalks, finely diced

2 carrots, peeled and finely diced

2 parsnips, peeled and diced

1 cup cipollini onions

2 sweet onions, finely diced

2 garlic cloves, minced

2 tablespoons tomato paste

4 strips of bacon, chopped

2 cups dry white wine

2 allspice berries

5 peppercorns

5 coriander seeds

2 bay leaves

3 sprigs of fresh thyme

1. Place 2 tablespoons of olive oil in a Dutch oven and warm it over medium heat. Season the rabbit with salt and pepper. Working in batches to avoid crowding the pot, add the rabbit to the pot and sear it until it is browned all over, about 5 minutes. Transfer the seared rabbit to a plate and set it aside.

2. Add the celery, carrots, parsnips, and onions and cook, stirring occasionally, until they have softened, about 5 minutes. Add the garlic and cook, stirring continually, for 1 minute.

3. Season the mixture with salt and pepper, stir in the tomato paste, bacon, and white wine, and bring the mixture to a simmer, scraping up any browned bits from the bottom of the pot.

4. Use a mortar and pestle to grind the allspice, peppercorns, and coriander seeds into a fine powder. Add the powder, bay leaves, thyme, and the rabbit to the Dutch oven, cover the pot, and reduce the heat to low. Cook until the rabbit is very tender, about 1 hour.

5. Season the stifado with salt and pepper and serve.

Rabbit in Sorrel Sauce

2½ lb. rabbit, cut into 8 pieces

Salt and pepper, to taste

2 tablespoons all-purpose flour

3 tablespoons extra-virgin olive oil

4 red onions, cut into wedges

2 garlic cloves, minced

1 cup dry white wine

1½ cups Chicken Stock (see page 253)

1 sprig of fresh rosemary

4 sprigs of fresh thyme

⅔ cup heavy cream

2 handfuls of fresh sorrel, chopped

1¼ lbs. small, waxy potatoes, peeled

2 tablespoons unsalted butter

Fresh parsley, chopped, for garnish

1. Preheat the oven to 350°F. Season the rabbit with salt and pepper and dust it with the flour. Place 2 tablespoons of the olive oil in a Dutch oven and warm it over medium heat. Add the rabbit and sear it until it is browned all over, turning it as necessary. Remove the rabbit from the pot and set it aside.

2. Add the onions and the remaining olive oil to the pot and cook, stirring occasionally, until they are translucent, about 3 minutes. Add the garlic and cook, stirring continually, for 1 minute.

3. Deglaze the pot with the wine, scraping up any browned bits from the bottom. Add the stock, rosemary, and thyme, return the rabbit to the pot, and cover the Dutch oven. Transfer it to the oven and braise the rabbit until it is tender, about 45 minutes, basting the rabbit occasionally.

4. While the rabbit is in the oven, place the potatoes in a large saucepan, cover them with water, and add salt. Bring the water to a boil and cook the potatoes until they are tender, about 20 minutes. Drain the potatoes and set them aside.

5. Remove the rabbit from the oven and then remove it and the herbs from the pot with a slotted spoon. Stir the cream into the pan juices and bring the sauce to a simmer over medium heat. Stir in the sorrel, return the rabbit to the pot, and cook until warmed through. Cover the pot and turn off the heat.

6. Place the butter in a large skillet and melt it over medium heat. Add the potatoes and fry them until they are lightly browned, 2 to 4 minutes, turning them as necessary.

7. Serve the rabbit over the potatoes, drizzle the sauce over the dish, and garnish with parsley.

Rabbit with Root Vegetables

3¼ lb. rabbit, cut into 8 pieces

2 tablespoons extra-virgin olive oil

Salt and pepper, to taste

3 carrots, peeled and sliced

2 parsnips, peeled and sliced

1 cup diced butternut squash

2 garlic cloves, minced

⅓ cup Roasted Chestnuts (see page 258)

3 bay leaves

2 sprigs of fresh rosemary

1 cup white wine

Fresh thyme, for garnish

1. Preheat the oven to 350°F. Place the rabbit in a Dutch oven, add the olive oil, season the rabbit with salt and pepper, and toss to coat. Add all of the remaining ingredients, except for the thyme, stir to combine, and cover the pot.

2. Place the pot in the oven and cook until the rabbit is tender and cooked through, about 1½ hours.

3. Turn off the oven and let the rabbit rest in the Dutch oven for 15 minutes.

4. Remove the pot from the oven, garnish the dish with thyme, and enjoy.

Rabbit Pie

1¾ lb. rabbit

2 garlic cloves, minced

1 tablespoon fresh thyme

Salt and pepper, to taste

1 cup dry red wine

1 tablespoon extra-virgin olive oil

1 large onion, diced

4½ cups sliced wild mushrooms

2 medium carrots, peeled and diced

1 celery stalk, chopped

1 cup Chicken Stock (see page 253)

1 package of frozen puff pastry, thawed

All-purpose flour, as needed

1 egg, beaten

1. Preheat the oven to 400°F. Rinse the rabbit under cold water and pat it dry with paper towels.

2. Place the rabbit in a roasting pan, sprinkle the garlic, thyme, salt, and pepper over it, and pour the wine into the pan. Cover the pan and place it in the oven. Braise the rabbit until it is cooked through and tender, 1½ to 2 hours.

3. While the rabbit is in the oven, place the olive oil in a large skillet and warm it over medium-high heat. Add the onion, mushrooms, carrots, and celery and cook, stirring occasionally, until the vegetables are tender, about 8 minutes. Remove the pan from heat and set the vegetables aside.

4. Remove the rabbit from the oven and let it cool briefly. Pick the meat off the bone, place it in a bowl, and stir in the vegetables and stock. Place the filling in the refrigerator and let it cool for 1 hour.

5. Preheat the oven to 375°F. Place the puff pastry on a flour-dusted work surface, roll it out, and cut out 2 crusts to fit an 8-inch pie plate.

6. Place the bottom crust in the pie plate. Spoon the filling into the crust, cover with the top crust, trim any excess, and crimp the edge to seal. Cut several slits in the top crust and brush it with the egg.

7. Place the pie in the oven and bake until the top crust is golden brown, about 35 minutes.

8. Remove the pie from the oven and let it cool briefly before serving.

Rabbit Roulade

2 garlic cloves, minced

2 tablespoons chopped fresh rosemary, plus more for garnish

¼ cup extra-virgin olive oil

Salt and pepper, to taste

1 large saddle of rabbit

8 strips of bacon

2 tablespoons all-purpose flour

1. Preheat the oven to 375°F. Place the garlic, rosemary, and 2 tablespoons of the olive oil in a bowl, season the mixture with salt and pepper, and stir to combine.

2. Remove any sinew from the rabbit saddle using the tip of a sharp knife. Butterfly the rabbit and season it with salt and pepper. Spread the garlic-and-rosemary mixture over the rabbit and lay half of the bacon over it. Roll the rabbit up along one of its long sides and wrap the remaining bacon around the outside of it. Secure the bacon with kitchen twine.

3. Dust the rabbit with the flour and season it with salt and pepper. Place the remaining olive oil in a roasting pan and warm it over medium heat. Add the rabbit to the pan and sear it until it is golden brown all over, turning the rabbit as needed.

4. Transfer the pan to the oven and roast the rabbit until it is firm to the touch, 8 to 10 minutes.

5. Remove the rabbit from the oven and let rest for 10 minutes. Slice the rabbit, garnish with additional rosemary, and enjoy.

Rabbit with Vegetables & Sage

3¼ lb. rabbit, cut into 8 pieces

Salt and pepper, to taste

2 tablespoons extra-virgin olive oil

1 cup dry white wine

2 red bell peppers, stems and seeds removed, chopped

4 tomatoes, chopped

2 onions, cut into wedges

2 garlic cloves, sliced

2 handfuls of spinach

1 cup Vegetable Stock (see page 251)

2 sprigs of fresh sage

1 bay leaf

1. Preheat the oven to 325°F. Season the rabbit generously with salt and pepper. Place the olive oil in a Dutch oven and warm it over medium heat. Working in batches to keep from crowding the pot, add the rabbit and sear it until it is browned all over.

2. Deglaze the pot with the wine, scraping up any browned bits from the bottom. Add the bell peppers, tomatoes, onions, garlic, and spinach, season the dish with salt and pepper, and stir in the stock.

3. Cover the pot and place it in the oven. Braise the rabbit for 40 minutes.

4. Add the sage and bay leaf and braise the rabbit until it is very tender, about 20 minutes.

5. Remove the rabbit from the oven, season it with salt and pepper, and serve.

Rabbit with Olives & Potatoes

½ cup all-purpose flour

3½ lb. rabbit, cut into 8 pieces

Salt and pepper, to taste

1 tablespoon unsalted butter

2 tablespoons extra-virgin olive oil

2 onions, sliced

2 large carrots, peeled and sliced

2 potatoes, peeled and cut into thin wedges

2 bay leaves

1 large lemon, sliced

½ cup pitted green olives

1 cup dry white wine

Fresh basil, torn, for garnish

1. Preheat the oven to 350°F. Place the flour in a shallow bowl, dredge the rabbit in it, and season the rabbit with salt and pepper.

2. Place the butter and olive oil in Dutch oven and warm the mixture over medium heat. Add the rabbit and cook it until it is browned all over, turning it as necessary. Remove the rabbit from the pot and set it aside.

3. Add the onions, carrots, potatoes, bay leaves, lemon slices, and a generous pinch of salt and pepper, and cook, stirring occasionally, until the vegetables and lemon are starting to brown, about 8 minutes.

4. Transfer the rabbit and vegetable mixture to a roasting pan. Arrange the olives around the rabbit and pour the wine over the dish. Place the pan in the oven and roast until the rabbit is cooked through and golden brown, 30 to 40 minutes.

5. Remove the pan from the oven, garnish the dish with basil, and enjoy.

Rabbit with Mustard

2 rabbit thighs

1 tablespoon kosher salt

4 tablespoons unsalted butter

1 tablespoon extra-virgin olive oil

2 large shallots, chopped

½ cup white wine

½ cup water

½ cup whole-grain mustard

1 teaspoon dried thyme

½ cup heavy cream

Fresh lemon thyme, for garnish

1. Season the rabbit with the salt. Place the butter in a large skillet and melt it over medium-high heat. Add the rabbit and sear until it is browned on each side, turning it as necessary. Transfer the rabbit to a plate and set it aside.

2. Add the olive oil and shallots to the pan and cook, stirring occasionally, until they have softened, about 5 minutes. Deglaze the pan with the wine, scraping up any browned bits from the bottom.

3. Stir in the water, mustard, and dried thyme and bring the liquid to a boil. Return the seared rabbit to the skillet and spoon the sauce over it. Reduce the heat to low, cover the pan, and simmer the rabbit until it is cooked through and almost falling off the bone, about 45 minutes.

4. Transfer the rabbit to a serving dish. Stir the heavy cream into the skillet and bring the sauce to a simmer. Pour the sauce over the rabbit, garnish the dish with lemon thyme, and enjoy.

Rabbit Bolognese

3 tablespoons extra-virgin olive oil

3 lb. rabbit, cut into 8 pieces

1 tablespoon kosher salt, plus more to taste

2 teaspoons black pepper, plus more to taste

2 onions, diced

1 carrot, peeled and diced

3 oz. pancetta, diced

3 garlic cloves, minced

1 cup dry red wine

2 tablespoons tomato paste

1 (14 oz.) can of diced tomatoes, with their liquid

1¼ cups Chicken Stock (see page 253)

1 lb. pasta

Fresh parsley, chopped, for garnish

1. Place the olive oil in a Dutch oven and warm it over medium-high heat. Season the rabbit with the salt and pepper, add it to the pot, and sear it until browned all over, turning it as necessary. Transfer the rabbit to a plate and set it aside.

2. Add the onions and carrot to the Dutch oven and cook, stirring occasionally, until they start to soften, about 4 minutes. Add the pancetta and cook until it is lightly browned. Add the garlic and cook, stirring continually, for 1 minute.

3. Return the rabbit to the pot, add the wine and tomato paste, and cook until liquid has reduced by about half. Stir in the tomatoes and stock and season the sauce with salt and pepper. Cover the pot, reduce the heat to medium-low, and cook until the rabbit is tender and can be shredded easily with a fork.

4. While the sauce is cooking, bring salted water to a boil in a large saucepan. Add the pasta and cook it until it is al dente, 6 to 8 minutes. Drain the pasta and set it aside.

5. Transfer the rabbit to a cutting board. Remove the meat from the bones and shred it. Stir the meat into the sauce and cook it for another minute.

6. Add the pasta to the sauce and toss to combine. Garnish the dish with parsley and enjoy.

FISH

Whether you fish with bait, flies, or lures, fishermen of every stripe can agree that there's no better way to spend a day than out on the water. And there's no better conclusion to that day then enjoying a meal featuring the light and fresh flavor of your catch.

Honey & Soy–Glazed Rainbow Trout

2 tablespoons honey

¼ cup soy sauce

2 large rainbow trout fillets, skin removed

Salt and pepper, to taste

2 tablespoons canola oil

2 cups green beans, trimmed

1 lime, halved

2 tablespoons sesame seeds, for garnish

1. Preheat the oven to 400°F. Line a baking sheet with parchment paper. Place the honey and soy sauce in a small bowl and stir until the honey has liquefied. Divide the glaze into two portions.

2. Place the trout on the baking sheet and brush it with half of the glaze. Season the trout with pepper and place it in the oven. Roast the trout until it is firm to the touch and slightly springy, about 10 minutes.

3. While the trout is in the oven, place the canola oil in a large skillet and warm it over high heat. Add the green beans, season them with salt and pepper, and stir-fry for 2 minutes. Cover the pan with a lid, reduce the heat to medium-low, and cook the green beans until they are tender, 2 to 3 minutes.

4. Remove the trout from the oven. Place it and the green beans on a serving platter, spoon the remaining glaze over the dish, and squeeze the lime over the top. Garnish the dish with sesame seeds and enjoy.

Rainbow Trout Jerky

1 lb. rainbow trout fillets

1 tablespoon brown sugar

1 tablespoon liquid smoke

1 teaspoon garlic powder

2 teaspoons kosher salt

1½ teaspoons black pepper

1. Slice the fillets lengthwise into ¼-inch-thick strips and cut each strip into 3- to 4-inch pieces.

2. Place the remaining ingredients in a mixing bowl and whisk until the sugar has dissolved and the mixture is thoroughly combined.

3. Add the trout to the marinade and stir until the strips are evenly coated.

4. Cover the bowl with plastic wrap, place it in the refrigerator, and marinate for at least 6 hours. If time allows, let it marinate overnight.

5. Remove the trout from the refrigerator and give it a stir.

6. To prepare the jerky in a dehydrator, arrange the trout on the dehydrator trays, making sure to leave space between each piece. Place it in the dehydrator, set it to 135°F, and dehydrate until the trout has dried out but is still flexible, 4 to 5 hours.

7. To prepare the jerky in an oven, preheat the oven to 150°F. Line two rimmed baking sheets with aluminum foil and place wire racks over the foil. Arrange the strips of trout on the racks, making sure to leave space between each piece and to keep the trout in a single layer. Place the pans in the oven and bake for 2 hours. Rotate the pans and then bake until the trout is dry to the touch, leathery, and slightly chewy, about 2 hours.

8. Remove the skin from the pieces of jerky. Store the jerky at room temperature in an airtight container, where it will keep for a few weeks. If you are interested in a longer shelf life for your jerky, place it in a bag and vacuum seal it. Stored in a cool, dry place, the vacuum-sealed jerky will keep for 6 months to 2 years.

FISH

Smoked Trout Tostadas

½ cup extra-virgin olive oil, plus more as needed

1 large white onion, sliced thin

4 garlic cloves, sliced

1 lb. smoked trout, flaked

2 teaspoons achiote powder

½ lb. carrots, peeled and grated

½ cup shredded cabbage

2 tablespoons chopped Castelvetrano olives

2 tablespoons fresh lemon juice

2 tablespoons kosher salt

4 Corn Tortillas (see page 265)

1. Place the olive oil in a large skillet and warm it over medium-low heat.

2. While the olive oil is warming up, coat another skillet with olive oil and warm it over medium heat. Add the onion and garlic and cook, stirring frequently, until the onion is translucent, about 3 minutes.

3. Stir the trout and achiote into the onion mixture and cook, stirring to break up the trout, until warmed through, about 3 minutes. Remove the pan from heat, stir in all of the remaining ingredients, except for the tortillas, and let the mixture sit.

4. Working with one tortilla at a time, fry the tortillas in the hot oil until they are crispy, 2 to 3 minutes. Transfer the tostadas to a paper towel–lined plate to drain.

5. Top each tostada with some of the smoked trout mixture and enjoy.

Teriyaki Salmon

3 tablespoons extra-virgin olive oil

4 Chinese eggplants, sliced into ½-inch pieces

1 red bell pepper, stem and seeds removed, sliced thin

2 tablespoons chopped scallions

1 cup bean sprouts

4 salmon fillets

Salt and pepper, to taste

¼ cup teriyaki sauce

1. Preheat the oven to 375°F. Place the olive oil in a large cast-iron skillet and warm it over medium-high heat. Add the eggplants, bell pepper, and scallions to the pan and cook, stirring occasionally, until the eggplants start to break down, about 5 minutes. Add the bean sprouts and stir to incorporate.

2. Place the salmon on top of the vegetables, skin side down, season with salt, pepper, and some of the teriyaki sauce, and transfer the pan to the oven. Bake until the salmon is cooked through, about 8 minutes.

3. Remove the pan from the oven, drizzle the remaining teriyaki sauce over the top, and serve.

Salmon Jerky

1 lb. salmon fillets

2 tablespoons fresh
lemon juice

1 tablespoon brown sugar

2 tablespoons liquid smoke

¼ cup tamari or soy sauce

1 teaspoon garlic powder

2 teaspoons kosher salt

1½ teaspoons black pepper

1. Using tweezers, remove the pinbones from the fillets. Leave the skin on, slice the fillets lengthwise into ¼-inch-thick strips, and cut each strip into 3- to 4-inch pieces.

2. Place the remaining ingredients in a mixing bowl and whisk until the sugar has dissolved and the mixture is thoroughly combined.

3. Add the salmon to the marinade and stir until the strips are evenly coated.

4. Cover the bowl with plastic wrap, place it in the refrigerator, and marinate for at least 6 hours. If time allows, let the meat marinate overnight.

5. Remove the salmon from the refrigerator and give it a stir.

6. To prepare the jerky in a dehydrator, arrange the salmon on the dehydrator trays, making sure to leave space between each piece. Place it in the dehydrator, set the temperature to 135°F, and dehydrate until the salmon has dried out but is still flexible, 6 to 8 hours.

7. To prepare the jerky in an oven, preheat the oven to 150°F. Line two rimmed baking sheets with aluminum foil and place wire racks over the foil. Arrange the strips on the racks, making sure to leave space between each piece and to keep the salmon in a single layer. Place the pans in the oven and bake for 2½ hours. Rotate the pans and then bake until the salmon is dry to the touch, leathery, and slightly chewy, 2½ to 3½ hours.

8. Remove the skin from the pieces of jerky. Store the jerky at room temperature in an airtight container, where it will keep for a few weeks. If you are interested in a longer shelf life for your jerky, place it in a bag and vacuum seal it. Stored in a cool, dry place, the vacuum-sealed jerky will keep for 6 months to 2 years.

FISH

Cedar-Plank Salmon

2 tablespoons whole-grain mustard

2 tablespoons mild honey or pure maple syrup

1 teaspoon chopped fresh rosemary

1 tablespoon lemon zest

½ teaspoon kosher salt

½ teaspoon black pepper

2 lb. skin-on salmon fillet (about 1½ inches thick)

1. Submerge a cedar grilling plank in water for 2 hours.

2. Prepare a gas or charcoal grill for medium-high heat (450°F).

3. In a bowl, combine the mustard, honey, rosemary, lemon zest, salt, and pepper and stir until well combined. Spread the mixture on the flesh of the salmon and let it stand at room temperature for 15 minutes.

4. Place the salmon on the plank, skin side down. Grill until the salmon is just cooked through and the edges are browned, 13 to 15 minutes.

5. Remove the salmon from the grill and let it rest on the plank for 3 minutes before slicing and serving.

Salmon & Vegetable Skewers

3½ tablespoons fresh lime juice

2 garlic cloves, minced

1 bunch of fresh parsley, chopped

2 tablespoons extra-virgin olive oil

Salt and pepper, to taste

1 lb. salmon fillets, skin removed, cut into large cubes

2 celery stalks, cut into 1-inch pieces

1 yellow bell pepper, stem and seeds removed and cut into 1-inch pieces

16 cherry tomatoes

Lime wedges, for serving

1. Prepare a gas or charcoal grill for medium heat (about 400°F). Place the lime juice, garlic, parsley, olive oil, salt, and pepper in a large bowl and stir until well combined. Add the salmon, celery, bell pepper, and tomatoes and toss until well coated. Cover the bowl with plastic wrap and let the mixture marinate in the refrigerator for 30 minutes.

2. Thread the salmon, celery, peppers, and tomatoes onto the skewers, alternating between them.

3. Place the skewers on the grill and cook until the salmon is cooked through, about 8 minutes, turning the skewers as needed.

4. Remove the skewers from the grill and serve with lime wedges.

Crispy Salmon Rice

2 tablespoons avocado oil

½ white onion, minced

¼ cup sliced scallions

¼ cup chopped fresh parsley

2 teaspoons kosher salt

2 cups leftover white rice

6 oz. salmon, chopped

1 tablespoon pomegranate molasses

1 tablespoon apple cider vinegar

1. Place the avocado oil in a large skillet and warm it over high heat. Add the onion, scallions, parsley, and salt and cook, stirring frequently, until the onion is translucent, about 3 minutes.

2. Add the rice and cook, stirring frequently, until the rice is crispy, 3 to 5 minutes. Add the salmon, reduce the heat to medium-high, and cook until the salmon is cooked through, about 4 minutes.

3. Place the pomegranate molasses and vinegar in a small bowl and whisk to combine. Add this mixture to the pan and stir until incorporated.

4. Remove the pan from heat and enjoy immediately.

Spinach, Fennel & Apple Salad with Smoked Trout

2 tablespoons white wine vinegar

1 tablespoon fresh lemon juice

1 tablespoon whole-grain mustard

1 teaspoon honey

½ cup extra-virgin olive oil

1 shallot, minced

2 teaspoons chopped fresh tarragon

Salt and pepper, to taste

4 cups baby spinach

2 Granny Smith apples, halved, core removed, sliced thin

1 fennel bulb, trimmed, core removed, and sliced thin

1 lb. smoked trout, skin removed, flaked

1. Place the vinegar, lemon juice, mustard, and honey in a salad bowl and whisk to combine. While whisking continually, slowly drizzle in the olive oil until it has emulsified. Stir in the shallot and tarragon and season the vinaigrette with salt and pepper.

2. Add the spinach, apples, and fennel to the salad bowl and toss to coat.

3. To serve, plate the salad, top each portion with some of the smoked trout, and enjoy.

Chilled Cucumber & Potato Soup with Smoked Salmon

1½ tablespoons unsalted butter

1 onion, chopped

4 cucumbers, peeled, seeds removed, and chopped

1 large russet potato, peeled and diced

3½ cups Chicken Stock (see page 253)

6 tablespoons chopped fresh dill

1 teaspoon kosher salt, plus more to taste

1 cup sour cream

4 oz. smoked salmon, chopped

1. Place the butter in a large saucepan and melt it over medium heat. Add the onion and cook, stirring occasionally, until it just softens, about 4 minutes.

2. Add the cucumbers and potato and cook, stirring continually, for 1 minute. Add the stock, 2 tablespoons of the dill, and the salt, raise the heat, and bring the soup to a boil.

3. Reduce the heat to low, cover the pan, and simmer the soup until the cucumbers and potato are tender, 20 to 25 minutes, stirring occasionally.

4. Transfer the soup to a food processor and blitz until it is smooth. Place the soup in a bowl and let it cool for 10 minutes.

5. Whisk in ½ cup of sour cream and the remaining dill. Cover the soup and chill it in the refrigerator for 3 hours.

6. Taste the soup, adjust the seasoning as necessary, and ladle the soup into bowls. Top each portion with a dollop of the remaining sour cream and some of the smoked salmon, and enjoy.

Smoked Trout Croquettes

1 lb. russet potatoes

¾ lb. smoked trout, flaked

Zest and juice of 1 lemon

1 garlic clove, grated

1 bunch of fresh chives, minced

Salt, to taste

Cayenne pepper, to taste

Canola oil, as needed

All-purpose flour, as needed

¼ cup mayonnaise

2 teaspoons Dijon mustard

1. Preheat the oven to 400°F. Line a baking sheet with parchment paper. Place the potatoes in the oven and bake until very tender, about 1 hour. Remove the potatoes from the oven, slice them in half, and let them cool.

2. Place the smoked trout in the work bowl of a stand mixer fitted with the paddle attachment. Add the lemon zest, garlic, and chives, season the mixture with salt and cayenne, and stir to combine. Remove the skin from the potatoes and use a potato ricer to press the flesh into the work bowl.

3. Beat the mixture until it is well combined and thick. Taste, adjust the seasoning as necessary, and form tablespoons of the mixture into balls. Place the balls on the parchment-lined baking sheet and chill them in the refrigerator for 1 hour.

4. Add canola oil to a Dutch oven until it is about 2 inches deep and warm it to 350°F. Place some flour in a shallow bowl. Remove the croquettes from the refrigerator and dredge them in the flour until lightly coated. Working in batches to avoid crowding the pot, gently slip the croquettes into the hot oil and fry them until golden brown, 3 to 4 minutes, turning them as necessary. Transfer the cooked croquettes to a paper towel–lined plate to drain.

5. Place the mayonnaise, mustard, and lemon juice in a small bowl and stir to combine. Serve this dipping sauce alongside the croquettes.

Smoked Trout Soup

1. Place the water, rice vinegar, and sugar in a small saucepan and bring the mixture to a boil. Remove the saucepan from heat and let the brine cool.

2. Place the enoki mushrooms in a mason jar, pour the brine over them, and let them sit as you prepare the soup.

3. Place the butter in a medium saucepan and melt it over medium heat. Add the onion and cook it over medium heat, stirring occasionally, until it is translucent, about 3 minutes.

4. Add the garlic, bell peppers, and Tabasco and cook, stirring frequently, for 2 minutes. Sprinkle the flour over the mixture and cook, stirring continually, for 3 minutes.

5. Stir in the stock, tomatoes, baby bella mushrooms, and milk and bring the soup to a boil. Reduce the heat so that the soup simmers and cook until the vegetables are tender, about 8 minutes.

6. Add the haddock and smoked trout and cook for 2 to 3 minutes. Add the mussels and cook until the majority of them have opened, about 5 minutes. Discard any mussels that did not open.

7. Season the soup with salt and pepper and ladle it into warmed bowls. Garnish with parsley and Gruyère and serve with crusty bread and the pickled mushrooms.

¼ cup water

¼ cup rice vinegar

¼ cup sugar

6 bunches of enoki mushrooms

2 tablespoons unsalted butter

1 onion, finely diced

1 garlic clove, minced

½ cup diced red bell pepper

½ cup diced green bell pepper

½ teaspoon Tabasco

¼ cup all-purpose flour

3 cups Fish Stock (see page 266)

1 (14 oz.) can of diced tomatoes, drained

1½ cups sliced baby bella mushrooms

1 cup milk

¾ lb. haddock fillets, chopped

4 oz. smoked trout, chopped

12 mussels, rinsed well and debearded

Salt and pepper, to taste

Fresh parsley, chopped, for garnish

Gruyère cheese, freshly grated, for garnish

Crusty bread, for serving

Lohikeitto

2 tablespoons unsalted butter

1 onion, diced

4 cups Fish Stock
(see page 266)

1 potato, peeled and diced

¾ lb. salmon fillet, skin
removed, chopped

1 cup heavy cream

Salt and pepper, to taste

Fennel fronds, for garnish

Fennel pollen, for garnish

Salmon roe, for garnish

Crème fraîche, for garnish

Toasted bread, for serving

1. Place the butter in a large saucepan and melt it over medium heat. Add the onion and cook, stirring occasionally, until it starts to soften, about 5 minutes.

2. Add the stock and bring the soup to a boil. Reduce the heat so that the soup simmers, add the potato, and cook until it is tender, 10 to 15 minutes.

3. Add the salmon and simmer until it is cooked through, about 3 minutes.

4. Stir in the heavy cream, season the soup with salt and pepper, and ladle it into warm bowls. Garnish each portion with fennel fronds, fennel pollen, salmon roe, and crème fraîche, and serve with toasted bread.

Beet-Cured Salmon

2 cups chopped beets

1 cup kosher salt

½ cup sugar

1 cup water

1 lb. salmon, skin removed, deboned

1. Place the beets, salt, and sugar in a food processor and pulse until the beets are finely chopped. Add the water in a slow stream and pulse until the mixture is a smooth puree.

2. Place the salmon in a baking dish and pour the puree over it. Place the salmon in the refrigerator and let it cure overnight.

3. Rinse the salmon under cold water. Place it on a wire rack set in a rimmed baking sheet and let it dry, uncovered, in the refrigerator overnight before serving.

APPENDIX

Beef Stock

7 lbs. beef bones, rinsed

4 cups chopped yellow onions

2 cups chopped carrots

2 cups chopped celery

3 garlic cloves, crushed

3 sprigs of fresh thyme

1 teaspoon black peppercorns

1 bay leaf

1. Place the beef bones in a stockpot and cover them with cold water. Bring to a simmer over medium-high heat and use a ladle to skim off any impurities that rise to the surface.

2. Add the remaining ingredients, reduce the heat to low, and simmer for 5 hours, occasionally skimming the stock to remove any impurities that rise to the surface.

3. Strain the stock, let it cool slightly, and transfer it to the refrigerator. Leave the stock uncovered and let it cool completely. Remove the layer of fat and cover. The stock will keep in the refrigerator for 3 to 5 days and in the freezer for up to 3 months.

Vegetable Stock

2 tablespoons extra-virgin olive oil

2 large leeks, trimmed and rinsed well

2 large carrots, peeled and sliced

2 celery stalks, sliced

2 large yellow onions, sliced

3 garlic cloves, unpeeled but smashed

2 sprigs of fresh parsley

2 sprigs of fresh thyme

1 bay leaf

8 cups water

½ teaspoon black peppercorns

Salt, to taste

1. Place the olive oil, leeks, carrots, celery, and onions in a large stockpot and cook over low heat until the liquid they release has evaporated. This will allow the flavor of the vegetables to become concentrated.

2. Add the garlic, parsley, thyme, bay leaf, water, peppercorns, and salt. Raise the heat to high and bring to a boil. Reduce the heat so that the stock simmers and cook for 2 hours, while skimming to remove any impurities that float to the surface.

3. Strain through a fine sieve, let the stock cool slightly, and place in the refrigerator, uncovered, to chill. Remove the fat layer and cover the stock. The stock will keep in the refrigerator for 3 to 5 days and in the freezer for up to 3 months.

Venison Stock

4 lbs. venison bones (neck and back bones), rinsed

4 cups chopped yellow onions

2 cups chopped carrots

2 cups chopped celery

3 garlic cloves, crushed

3 sprigs of fresh thyme

1 teaspoon black peppercorns

1 bay leaf

1. Place the venison bones in a stockpot and cover them with cold water. Bring to a simmer over medium-high heat and use a ladle to skim off any impurities that rise to the surface.

2. Add the remaining ingredients, reduce the heat to low, and simmer for 5 hours, occasionally skimming the stock to remove any impurities that rise to the surface.

3. Strain the stock, let it cool slightly, and transfer it to the refrigerator. Leave the stock uncovered and let it cool completely. Remove the layer of fat and cover. The stock will keep in the refrigerator for 3 to 5 days and in the freezer for up to 3 months.

Chicken Stock

7 lbs. chicken bones, rinsed

4 cups chopped yellow onions

2 cups chopped carrots

2 cups chopped celery

3 garlic cloves, crushed

3 sprigs of fresh thyme

1 teaspoon black peppercorns

1 bay leaf

1. Place the chicken bones in a stockpot and cover them with cold water. Bring to a simmer over medium-high heat and use a ladle to skim off any impurities that rise to the surface.

2. Add the remaining ingredients, reduce the heat to low, and simmer for 5 hours, skimming the stock occasionally to remove any impurities that rise to the surface.

3. Strain the stock, let it cool slightly, and transfer it to the refrigerator. Leave the stock uncovered and let it cool completely. Remove the layer of fat and cover. The stock will keep in the refrigerator for 3 to 5 days and in the freezer for up to 3 months.

Mushroom Stock

2 tablespoons extra-virgin olive oil

3 lbs. mushrooms

1 onion, chopped

1 garlic clove, minced

2 bay leaves

1 tablespoon black peppercorns

2 sprigs of fresh thyme

1 cup white wine

8 cups water

1. Place the olive oil and mushrooms in a large stockpot and cook over low heat, stirring occasionally, for 30 to 40 minutes. The longer you cook the mushrooms, the better the stock will taste, as the lengthy cook time concentrates the flavor.

2. Add the onion, garlic, bay leaves, peppercorns, and thyme and cook, stirring occasionally, for 5 minutes. Add the white wine, cook for 5 minutes, and then add the water.

3. Raise the heat and bring the stock to a boil. Reduce the heat so that the stock simmers and cook for 2 to 3 hours, until you are pleased with the taste. Strain through a fine sieve, discard the solids, and refrigerate the stock until cool. The stock will keep in the refrigerator for 3 to 5 days and in the freezer for up to 3 months.

Roasted Garlic

6 heads of garlic

Extra-virgin olive oil,
as needed

Salt, to taste

1. Preheat the oven to 375°F. Cut the top off each head of garlic and place the heads of garlic, cut side up, in a baking dish that is small enough for them to fit snugly. Add about ¼ inch of water to the dish, drizzle olive oil over the garlic, and sprinkle with salt.

2. Cover the dish with aluminum foil, place it in the oven, and roast for 20 minutes. Lift the foil and test to see if the garlic is tender and browned. If not, re-cover the dish, add water if it has evaporated, and roast for another 10 minutes. Remove from the oven and use as desired.

Clarified Butter

1 cup unsalted butter

1. Place the butter in a saucepan and melt it over medium heat.

2. Reduce the heat to the lowest possible setting. Cook until the butter fat is very clear and the milk solids have dropped to the bottom of the pan.

3. Skim the foam from the surface of the butter and discard it. Strain the clarified butter into a container and refrigerate until ready to use.

Ras el Hanout

1 teaspoon turmeric

1 teaspoon ground ginger

1 teaspoon cumin

¾ teaspoon cinnamon

1 teaspoon black pepper

½ teaspoon coriander

½ teaspoon cayenne pepper

½ teaspoon allspice

½ teaspoon freshly grated nutmeg

¼ teaspoon ground cloves

1 teaspoon fine sea salt

1. Place all of the ingredients in a bowl, stir to combine, and use immediately or store in an airtight container.

Roasted Chestnuts

1 lb. chestnuts

½ teaspoon kosher salt

¼ teaspoon black pepper

2 tablespoons unsalted butter, melted

1 tablespoon extra-virgin olive oil

3 sprigs of fresh thyme

1 cinnamon stick

2 whole cloves

1. Preheat the oven to 425°F. Carve an "X" on the rounded side of each chestnut and place them in a bowl of hot water. Soak for about 10 minutes.

2. Drain the chestnuts and create an aluminum foil pouch. Place the chestnuts in the pouch, sprinkle the salt and pepper over them, drizzle the butter and olive oil over the top, and add the thyme, cinnamon stick, and cloves to the pouch. Close the pouch, leaving an opening so that steam can escape.

3. Place the chestnuts in the oven and roast until tender, 40 to 45 minutes. Remove the chestnuts from the oven, remove the meats from the shell, and serve them warm.

BBQ Sauce

1 tablespoon extra-virgin olive oil

4 garlic cloves, minced

1 cup ketchup

¼ cup water

2 tablespoons molasses

2 tablespoons dark brown sugar

1 tablespoon apple cider vinegar

1 tablespoon Worcestershire sauce

1 bay leaf

1 teaspoon mustard powder

1 teaspoon chili powder

1 teaspoon onion powder

1 teaspoon liquid smoke

1 teaspoon black pepper

1 teaspoon kosher salt

1. Place the olive oil in a saucepan and warm it over medium-high heat. Add the garlic and cook, stirring continually, for 1 minute.

2. Stir in the remaining ingredients and bring the sauce to a boil. Reduce the heat to medium and simmer until the sauce has reduced by one-third, about 20 minutes.

3. Remove the bay leaf and discard it. Taste, adjust the seasoning if necessary, and use immediately, or let the sauce cool and store it in the refrigerator.

Spätzle

2½ cups all-purpose flour

1 tablespoon kosher salt, plus more to taste

2 large eggs

1¼ cups whole milk, plus more as needed

1. Place the flour, salt, eggs, and milk in a mixing bowl and stir until the dough becomes somewhat shiny and resembles pancake batter, 7 to 8 minutes. If the dough seems too thick, incorporate more milk, 1 teaspoon at a time. Cover the bowl with plastic wrap and let the dough rest at room temperature for 1 hour.

2. Bring a large pot of salted water to a boil and prepare an ice water bath. Reduce the heat so the water is gently boiling. Working in batches, place handfuls of dough into the cup of a spätzle maker that has been coated with nonstick cooking spray. While pressing down, grate the dough into the boiling water and cook until the spätzle float to the top, 2 to 3 minutes. Stir occasionally to prevent the spätzle from sticking to the bottom.

3. Remove the cooked spätzle with a slotted spoon and transfer them to the ice water bath. When all of the spätzle are cooked, place them on paper towels to dry. When dry, use as desired.

Apricot Jam

2 lbs. apricots, halved, pitted, and chopped

Zest and juice of 1 lemon

2 lbs. sugar

1 cup water

1 tablespoon unsalted butter

1. Place all the ingredients, except for the butter, in a large saucepan and bring to a gentle boil over medium heat, stirring to help the sugar dissolve. Boil the mixture for about 5 minutes.

2. Reduce the heat and simmer for 15 minutes, stirring frequently. If you prefer a smoother jam, mash the mixture with a wooden spoon as it cooks.

3. When the jam has formed a thin skin, remove the pan from the heat. Add the butter and stir to disperse any froth. Let the jam cool completely before using or storing in the refrigerator.

Baguettes

5 oz. water

11½ oz. bread flour, plus more as needed

½ oz. whole wheat flour

1 teaspoon sugar

1 cup sourdough starter

1 tablespoon kosher salt

1. Place the water, flours, and sugar in the work bowl of a stand mixer fitted with the dough hook and work the mixture at low speed for 6 minutes. Remove the bowl from the mixer and cover it with plastic wrap. Let the dough sit at room temperature for 1 hour to allow the dough to autolyse.

2. Place the work bowl back on the mixer and add the starter and salt. Knead the mixture at low speed until the dough starts to come together, about 2 minutes. Increase the speed to medium and knead until the dough is elastic and pulls away from the side of the bowl.

3. Shape the dough into a ball and spray the seam side with water. Dust a 9-inch banneton (proofing basket) with flour. Place the dough in the proofing basket, seam side down. Cover the bread with plastic wrap and let it sit on the counter for 2 hours.

4. Place the dough on a flour-dusted work surface, divide it in half, and shape each piece into a ball. Cover the dough with a moist linen towel and let it sit on the counter for 15 minutes.

5. Punch down the pieces of dough until they are rough ovals. Working with one piece at a time, take the side closest to you and roll it away from you. Starting halfway up, fold in the corners and roll the dough into a rough baguette shape.

6.   Place both hands over one piece of dough. Gently roll the dough while moving your hands back and forth over it and gently pressing down until it is about 16 inches long. Repeat with the other piece of dough.

7.   Place the baguettes on a baguette pan, cover with plastic wrap, and chill them in the refrigerator overnight.

8.   Remove the baguettes from the refrigerator, place the pan in a naturally warm spot, and let it sit for 2 hours.

9.   Preheat the oven to 450°F.

10. Using a very sharp knife, cut four slits at a 45-degree angle along the length of each baguette.

11. Place the baguettes in the oven, spray the oven with 5 spritzes of water, and bake until the baguettes are a deep golden brown, 20 to 30 minutes.

12. Remove the baguettes from the oven, place them on a wire rack, and let them cool slightly before slicing.

Tapenade

½ cup finely chopped
Kalamata olives

1 teaspoon capers, drained,
rinsed, and finely chopped

1 teaspoon finely chopped
sun-dried tomatoes in
olive oil

1 teaspoon dried oregano

1. Combine all of the ingredients in a mixing bowl and serve
immediately.

Corn Tortillas

1 lb. masa harina

1½ tablespoons kosher salt

3 cups warm filtered water, plus more as needed

1. In the work bowl of stand mixer fitted with the paddle attachment, combine the masa harina and salt. With the mixer on low speed, slowly begin to add the water. The mixture should come together as a soft, smooth dough. You want the masa to be moist enough so that when a small ball of it is pressed flat in your hands the edges do not crack. Also, the masa should not stick to your hands when you peel it off your palm.

2. Let the masa rest for 10 minutes and check the hydration again. You may need to add more water depending on environmental conditions.

3. Warm a cast-iron skillet over high heat. Portion the masa into 1-ounce balls and cover them with a damp linen towel.

4. Line a tortilla press with two 8-inch circles of plastic. You can use a grocery store bag, a resealable bag, or even a standard kitchen trash bag as a source for the plastic. Place a masa ball in the center of one circle and gently push down on it with the palm of one hand to flatten. Place the other plastic circle on top and then close the tortilla press, applying firm, even pressure to flatten the masa into a round tortilla.

5. Open the tortilla press and remove the top layer of plastic. Carefully pick up the tortilla and remove the bottom piece of plastic.

6. Gently lay the tortilla flat in the pan, taking care to not wrinkle it. Cook for 15 to 30 seconds, until the edge begins to lift up slightly. Turn the tortilla over and let it cook for 30 to 45 seconds before turning it over one last time. If the hydration of the masa was correct and the heat is high enough, the tortilla should puff up and inflate. Remove the tortilla from the pan and store in a tortilla warmer lined with a linen towel. Repeat until all of the prepared masa has been made into tortillas.

Fish Stock

¼ cup extra-virgin olive oil

1 leek, trimmed, rinsed well, and chopped

1 large yellow onion, unpeeled, root cleaned, chopped

2 large carrots, chopped

1 celery stalk, chopped

¾ lb. whitefish bodies

4 sprigs of fresh parsley

3 sprigs of fresh thyme

2 bay leaves

1 teaspoon black peppercorns

1 teaspoon kosher salt

8 cups water

1. Place the olive oil in a stockpot and warm it over low heat. Add the vegetables and cook until the liquid they release has evaporated.

2. Add the remaining ingredients to the pot, raise the heat to high, and bring to a boil. Reduce the heat so that the stock simmers and cook for 3 hours, skimming to remove any impurities that float to the surface.

3. Strain the stock through a fine sieve, let it cool slightly, and place in the refrigerator, uncovered, to chill. When the stock is completely cool, remove the fat layer from the top and cover. The stock will keep in the refrigerator for 3 to 5 days and in the freezer for up to 3 months.

Bouquet Garni

2 bay leaves

3 sprigs of fresh thyme

3 sprigs of fresh parsley

1. Cut a 2-inch section of kitchen twine. Tie one side of the twine around the herbs and knot it tightly.

2. To use, attach the other end of the twine to one of the pot's handles and slip the herbs into the broth. Remove before serving.

Classic Dumplings

2 cups all-purpose flour

1 teaspoon baking powder

1 teaspoon kosher salt

1 tablespoon extra-virgin olive oil

2 eggs

¾ cup water

2 tablespoons minced fresh chives

1. Place the flour, baking powder, and salt in a mixing bowl and whisk to combine.

2. Add the olive oil, eggs, water, and chives and stir the mixture with a fork until it comes together as a loose dough. Add tablespoons of the dough to a simmering soup or sauce and cook the dumplings until they are cooked through, 6 to 8 minutes.

YIELD: 4 SERVINGS / ACTIVE TIME: 15 MINUTES / TOTAL TIME: 25 MINUTES

WILD GAME COOKING

268

Rose Hip Syrup

1 lb. rose hips, trimmed

3 cups water

¾ lb. sugar

1. Place the rose hips in a food processor and blitz until smooth.

2. Place the rose hip puree in a saucepan, add the water, and bring the mixture to a boil. Reduce the heat and simmer the mixture for 15 minutes.

3. Line a fine-mesh sieve with cheesecloth and strain the rose hip juice through it. Discard the solids, rinse off the cheesecloth, and strain the juice once more.

4. Place the rose hip juice in a saucepan and bring it to a boil. Add the sugar and cook, stirring to dissolve. Remove the pan from heat and let the syrup cool completely before using or storing.

Gnocchi

3 lbs. Yukon Gold potatoes

2 large eggs

2½ cups all-purpose flour, plus more as needed

1 tablespoon kosher salt

1. Preheat the oven to 400°F. Place the potatoes on a baking sheet, prick them several times with a fork, and bake until they are soft all the way through, about 1 hour. Remove from the oven, slice them open, and let cool completely.

2. When the potatoes are cool enough to handle, scoop the flesh into a mixing bowl and mash until smooth. Make a well in the center of the potatoes and add the eggs, 1½ cups of the flour, and the salt. Work the mixture with your hands to combine and then add the remaining flour in small increments. Knead the dough to incorporate and stop adding flour as soon as the dough holds together and is no longer sticky.

3. Place a handful of dough on a flour-dusted work surface and roll it into a ¾-inch-thick rope with your hands. Repeat with the remaining dough.

4. Cut the ropes into ½-inch-wide pieces and roll the gnocchi over the tines of a fork (or a gnocchi board) while gently pressing down to create ridges. If the gnocchi start sticking to the fork, dip it into flour before pressing the gnocchi against it. Place the shaped gnocchi on a parchment-lined baking sheet, lightly dust them with flour, and use as desired.

Pita Bread

1 cup lukewarm water (90°F)

1 tablespoon active dry yeast

1 tablespoon sugar

1¾ cups all-purpose flour, plus more as needed

1 cup whole wheat flour

1 tablespoon kosher salt

1. In a large mixing bowl, combine the water, yeast, and sugar. Let the mixture sit until it starts to foam, about 15 minutes.

2. Add the flours and salt and work the mixture until it comes together as a smooth dough. Cover the bowl with a linen towel and let it rise for about 15 minutes.

3. Preheat the oven to 500°F and place a baking stone on the floor of the oven.

4. Divide the dough into eight pieces and form them into balls. Place the balls on a flour-dusted work surface, press them down, and roll them until they are about ¼ inch thick.

5. Working with one pita at a time, place the pita on the baking stone and bake until it is puffy and brown, about 8 minutes. Remove from the oven and serve warm or at room temperature.

Naan

1 teaspoon active dry yeast

½ cup warm water (105°F)

11½ oz. all-purpose flour

½ cup full-fat yogurt

3 tablespoons canola oil

Unsalted butter, melted, for topping

1. Combine the yeast and water in a small bowl, gently stir, and let the mixture rest until it starts to foam, about 10 minutes.

2. Place the yeast mixture and the remaining ingredients, except for the melted butter, in the work bowl of a stand mixer fitted with the paddle attachment and work the mixture until it comes together as a smooth dough, about 10 minutes. Cover the work bowl with plastic wrap and let the dough rest in a naturally warm spot until it has doubled in size, about 1 hour.

3. Line a baking sheet with plastic wrap. Place the dough on a flour-dusted work surface, divide it into 8 pieces, and shape them into rounds. Place the rounds on the baking sheet, cover them with plastic wrap, and let them rest for 30 minutes.

4. Warm a cast-iron skillet over medium-high heat. Coat the skillet with nonstick cooking spray, flatten one of the rounds, and place it in the pan. Cook until it is browned and bubbly on both sides, 2 to 3 minutes per side.

5. Remove the cooked naan from the pan, brush it with melted butter, and let it cool on wire rack. Repeat with the remaining pieces of dough.

Tomato Sauce

2 tablespoons avocado oil

1 large garlic clove, chopped

1 teaspoon grated fresh ginger

1 cinnamon stick

1 (28 oz.) can of chopped San Marzano tomatoes, with their liquid

½ teaspoon cumin

¼ teaspoon coriander

⅛ teaspoon cayenne pepper

1. Place the avocado oil in a large saucepan and warm it over medium heat. Add the garlic and ginger and cook, stirring frequently, until the mixture is fragrant, about 1 minute.

2. Add the cinnamon stick and cook, stirring continually, for 30 seconds. Add the remaining ingredients and bring the sauce to a boil.

3. Reduce the heat and simmer the sauce until the flavor has developed to your liking, about 30 minutes.

4. Remove the cinnamon stick from the sauce and use as desired or store in the refrigerator.

Pear & Cranberry Chutney

¾ lb. cranberries

2 pears, peeled, cores removed, diced

½ cup honey

1 cup water

1. Place all of the ingredients in a saucepan and bring the mixture to a boil over high heat.

2. Reduce the heat to low and simmer the chutney until the cranberries begin to burst, about 15 minutes.

3. Remove the pan from heat and let the chutney cool completely before using or storing.

Metric Conversion Chart

U.S. Measurement	Approximate Metric Liquid Measurement	Approximate Metric Dry Measurement
1 teaspoon	5 ml	—
1 tablespoon or ½ ounce	15 ml	14 g
1 ounce or ⅛ cup	30 ml	29 g
¼ cup or 2 ounces	60 ml	57 g
⅓ cup	80 ml	—
½ cup or 4 ounces	120 ml	113 g
⅔ cup	160 ml	—
¾ cup or 6 ounces	180 ml	—
1 cup or 8 ounces or ½ pint	240 ml	227 g
1½ cups or 12 ounces	350 ml	—
2 cups or 1 pint or 16 ounces	475 ml	454 g
3 cups or 1½ pints	700 ml	—
4 cups or 2 pints or 1 quart	950 ml	—

INDEX

About Cider Mill Press
Book Publishers

Good ideas ripen with time. From seed to harvest, Cider Mill Press brings fine reading, information, and entertainment together between the covers of its creatively crafted books. Our Cider Mill bears fruit twice a year, publishing a new crop of titles each spring and fall.

"Where Good Books Are Ready for Press"

501 Nelson Place
Nashville, TN 37214

cidermillpress.com